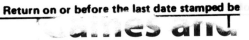

Activities

Other Books of Interest from A & C Black

Swimming Games and Activities

*for individuals, partners
and groups of children*

Jim Noble and Alan Cregeen

Second edition

A & C Black • London

Published by A & C Black (Publishers) Ltd
37 Soho Square, London WID 3QZ
www.acblack.com

First edition 1988
Second edition 1999, Reprinted 1993, 2002

© 1988 Alan Cregeen and Jim Noble
Additional material for second edition
© 1999 Jim Noble

ISBN 0 7136 5204 7

A & C Black uses paper produced with elemental chlorine-free pulp, harvested from managed sustainable forests.

A CIP catalogue record for this book is available from the British Library.

Acknowledgements
The authors would like to thank Ruth C. Birrell for preparing the illustrations for the first edition of *Swimming Games and Activities*, and George Austin, for the additional illustrations for the second edition. The survival swimming illustrations in Chapter 8 are drawn from material supplied by the Amateur Swimming Association.

Cover photograph by Denis O'Clair/Tony Stone Images.

Note
Whilst every effort has been made to ensure that the content of this book is as technically accurate and as sound as possible, neither the author nor publisher can accept responsibility for any injury or loss sustained as a result of the use of this material.

Typeset in 11 on 12pt Minion

Printed and bound in Great Britain by
Bell & Bain Limited, Thornliebank, Scotland

Contents

Preface to the Second Edition

This new edition of *Swimming Games and Activities* has been updated and now contains well over 200 activities and games for children, designed to help them gain water confidence and develop their swimming skills.

In addition to describing many new activities, details of incentive awards are provided in the form of graded tests for non-swimmers, together with distance tests for beginners and the more proficient swimmers. There is also a completely new section on survival swimming.

It is hoped that those parents or teachers who make use of this book will find the material helps to make their tuition enjoyable and stimulating for both their children and themselves.

Finally, since this book was last revised, my co-author, Alan Cregeen, has passed away. For over 40 years he played an important role in the educational work of the Amateur Swimming Association, latterly as a Principal Tutor, and in that capacity and as a Physical Education Organiser in Lancashire County and Trafford, he did much to promote the sport of swimming. His contribution will be sadly missed.

Jim Noble
August 1999

Foreword to the First Edition

Play is the powerful process by which the young of all the animal kingdom acquire the skills they will need as adults. Unenlightened people may dismiss play as 'childish', but it is really 'child-like'. As Sigmund Freud said, no one should 'underestimate the importance of play'.

The authors of this book, both of whom have unrivalled expertise in the teaching of swimming and who have been members of the Education Committee of the Amateur Swimming Association for many years, recognise in full the vital role of play in the development of swimming techniques.

Swimming teachers will be able to choose from a vast collection of attractive material stimulating games and activities that can be used to enhance swimming lessons and to enable pupils to become confident and skilful in the water.

Cyril Meek
President of the Physical Education
Association of Great Britain and Ireland

Introduction

Several theories have been advanced to explain the origins, purpose and significance of play. However, it is self-evident that children do like to play and it is generally recognised that they can learn through play activity, much of which will be self-initiated. In their free play they gain experience of the world around them and try out activities which will, no doubt, assume greater significance for them at a later stage in their development. In these early stages of learning, style and technique are of minor importance, whereas enjoyment and achievement are of much greater relevance.

In the controlled situation of a swimming lesson, the enterprising and perceptive teacher will take advantage of this natural impulse to play, wisely guiding it into useful channels of development so that often the children learn almost without realising it.

In the early stages of learning to swim there is sufficient enjoyment and challenge in coming to terms with the water and discovering its supportive nature. Then, as confidence grows and personal skill develops, activity can extend to co-operating with or competing against others. Play becomes more organised and games will gradually develop, assuming greater importance in the learning situation.

It is assumed that most readers will be familiar with the teaching of swimming and the methods of developing sound stroke techniques. What is offered, in the chapters which follow, is a range of play activities and games which may be used to introduce pupils to the experience of moving about in water to supplement on-going teaching and to add to their repertoire of enjoyable water activities.

NOTE

Although this book is intended not only for the use of teachers but also of swimming instructors, club leaders, parents and others, for ease of reference the term 'teacher' has been adopted throughout to describe the person in charge of the group or class.

Individuals are also referrred to as 'he', but this should be taken to mean 'he' or 'she' where appropriate.

1 • Safety Precautions

GENERAL RULES

Closeness to water always presents potential hazards and for this reason the need for safety precautions cannot be overstressed. Although some of these may appear obvious, it should be remembered that accidents and drownings do sometimes occur, even in indoor swimming pools, and that they usually result from inadequate supervision or failure to follow common-sense rules.

It is important, therefore, to ensure that certain safety rules are clearly understood and followed during all swimming lessons and it is recommended that the following be regarded as the minimum number of points to note:

- There should be no running on the poolside – slipping can cause personal injury or injury to others.
- No one should be allowed to enter the water until permission has been given.
- Before jumping in or diving, a check should be made to see that the water is clear.
- Rough play, e.g. pushing others into the water or ducking them, should not be permitted.
- There must be prompt obedience to a whistle or to any other signal used by the person in charge to indicate a stoppage of activity or to gain attention.
- Sweets or chewing gum should be banned during swimming lessons.
- If any apparatus is required, it should be checked to make sure it is in sound condition and it should be returned to safe storage after use.

Those in charge should also be familiar with the emergency measures applicable to the pool. These will include knowing where rescue equipment and resuscitation apparatus are kept and the location of the emergency telephone or bell.

Non-swimmers and beginners should remain in shallow water where they can stand or walk confidently and in complete safety. For this reason a 'safe area' should be designated and preferably roped off from the rest of the pool.

Once pupils have become waterborne and are able to achieve near horizontal positions in the water, it is important that they should be able to recover to a balanced standing position in the water from both prone and supine floating. They should also be able to rotate from a position on the front (prone) to a position on the back (supine) and vice versa. Furthermore, since pupils in play and game situations may move off balance, it is important that they should know how to reorientate themselves in the water.

RECOVERY SKILLS

The following skills are included here as a reminder and to emphasise their importance.

Regaining the standing position from prone floating (see fig. l)
Recovery is achieved quite simply by lifting the head, tucking the knees towards the chest,

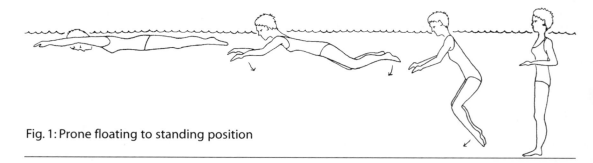

Fig. 1: Prone floating to standing position

pressing downwards in the water with both hands and pushing the feet downwards to the floor of the pool.

Regaining the standing position from supine floating *(see fig. 2)*

From this position, the arms are first pressed downwards and backwards, then moved forwards as though skipping backwards. At the same time the head is lifted forwards and the knees are brought forwards towards the chest. In consequence the body rotates into a vertical position, the feet are planted firmly on the floor of the pool and the arms are moved outwards in order to assist balance.

When practising in pairs, the supporter takes up a position behind a partner, placing the hands beneath the partner's shoulders and exerting gentle pressure to assist standing.

Rotating

a) Sideways: from a prone or supine floating position, raise the hip and shoulder on one side, turning the head in the same direction.

b) Forwards or backwards: from a prone or supine floating position, raise the head, then tuck the body by drawing the knees towards the chest, causing the body to rotate. Stretch out as soon as the body has passed through the upright position.

For both of these skills, sculling movements of the hands and arms may be used to assist the rotation and to control body balance.

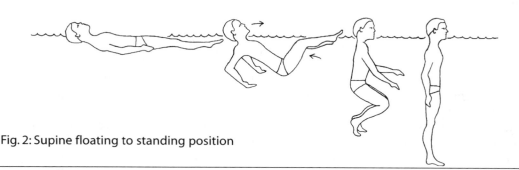

Fig. 2: Supine floating to standing position

2 • Organisation

WHEN TO PLAY

The use of play activities and games will be at the discretion of the teacher, in accordance with the prevailing circumstances and the development of the swimming programme. Although there is no set place in the lesson when they might be included, the following are possibilities:

- when introducing pupils to the water on their first visits
- as a 'warm-up' or introductory activity in any lesson
- as a contrasting activity or 'break' in a lesson or during training
- as a group activity in a schedule-type lesson
- as a 'winding down' or concluding activity
- as a complete games lesson
- as events in a swimming gala
- as preparatory stages in the development of specific skills or games, e.g. turns, water polo or synchronised swimming.

SELECTION OF ACTIVITIES

In the early stages, activities should be aimed at developing the feel of water support all round the body and an appreciation that pressing against the water with the limbs will not only assist balance but also provide propulsion.

As far as possible, consistent with the constraints of the activities themselves, pupils should be immersed in water not less than chest deep and preferably up to the shoulders, otherwise there is little relationship with the development of swimming which takes place through, and not over, the water. These fundamentals should always be borne in mind when selecting games or activities, which should bear some relationship with the development of swimming skills.

- Where possible, attempt to relate the chosen activities to the theme of the lesson.
- Consider all fundamental aspects of swimming – balance, breathing, buoyancy and propulsion, and vary the activities both during a lesson and from one lesson to another.
- Time permitting, include individual, partner and group activities. Working in groups can be reassuring for some timid pupils, thus building up their confidence.

MODIFICATIONS

Many of the activities will call for some ingenuity on the part of the teacher, depending upon the needs of the pupils and the prevailing situations:

- the level of the class or group – whether the members are non-swimmers, beginners or swimmers
- the size and shape of the pool and the methods of organising the space available
- the extent of the shallow and deep areas of water
- the temperature of the water
- the availability of apparatus
- the number of pupils involved.

MAINTAINING INTEREST AND ENJOYMENT

It is important to consider the abilities of the pupils and to ensure that all of them have a reasonable chance of achievement. Avoid playing any games for too long and be alert for signs of tiredness, boredom and frustration. Although teaching points should be made where appropriate, they should be succinct and should not interfere unduly with the flow of activity.

Games involving elimination tend to penalise those who are lacking in confidence or skill and can lead to feelings of incompetence or rejection. Elimination also deprives participants, albeit temporarily, of the enjoyable learning experience which is being offered.

KEEPING WARM

The use of small teams will help to provide maximum activity and involvement, avoiding unnecessary waiting for turns, especially in relay-type activities.

If elimination games are introduced, those who are eliminated should be provided with some appropriate activity to perform so that they remain active and do not become cold or bored.

Explanations should be brief, clear and concise, enabling the activity to start quickly.

DISTINGUISHING TEAMS

Some games will require the players to wear distinguishing colours or team indicators. In land-based games it is customary for jerseys, distinctive T-shirts, training bibs or coloured braids to be worn, but in water none of these methods is practicable. Alternative possibilities are as follows:

- the wearing of coloured caps (cloth or rubber)
- the use of coloured rubber bands worn on the wrist (some swimming pools adopt this system during public sessions for the allocation of lockers in changing-rooms)
- DIY elastic arm bands can be made (these should be wide enough to be readily seen)
- for some activities players might be distinguished by wearing just one arm band, though this may restrict movement through the water, particularly when orthodox swimming movements are involved.

In team events it should only be necessary for one of the teams to wear distinguishing colours.

ORGANISATION OF SPACE

On land, painted lines and chalk marks can be used to indicate playing areas of courts, but in the swimming pool the marking of spaces presents difficulties. However, with some ingenuity on the part of the teacher the problem can be overcome, as the following suggestions indicate:

- when players are required to maintain a certain distance apart, use can be made of the lane markings on the bottom of the pool. Most pools have these in the form of coloured tiles
- pieces of apparatus or markings on the poolside can be used to indicate where teams should line up
- players can be distanced by having a thrower in the middle of the pool, with the catchers standing with their backs close to the poolside
- though many pools have lane ropes which stretch from end to end, these may be too cumbersome to be used across the pool. Instead, shorter lengths of floating rope

can be used to mark off the pool into sections. To make the ropes more noticeable, plastic containers can be attached at intervals

- players can be kept in reasonable circular formation by placing a plastic hoop in the middle and using this as a focal point from which they can maintain a prescribed distance. Alternatively, buoyant rope can be arranged in a circular shape in the water.

APPARATUS

If any apparatus or small items of equipment are used, they should be prepared beforehand and placed round the poolside within easy reach of the players when required. At the end of the session they should be returned tidily so that they are readily available for subsequent users. Apparatus should be checked regularly for safety and possible damage in use. Any improvised apparatus should be safe to use and handle.

CLASSIFICATION OF PUPILS

- **Non-swimmer** has not yet become waterborne and still has to maintain contact with the bottom of the pool.

- **Beginner** is able to move through the water using very basic stroke movements, either on the front or on the back, and is able to regain a standing position.
- **Swimmer** uses a clearly recognisable stroke, or strokes, with appropriate breathing and is able to cover a minimum distance of 25 metres.

ACTIVITIES

Activities for non-swimmers and beginners are intended to be performed in shallow water. However, it is possible to adapt many such activities for use by swimmers in deeper water. Examples of such adaptations will be found in chapter 4.

GRADED TESTS AND INCENTIVE AWARDS

Those in charge of classes of non-swimmers may find the progressive tests listed in Appendix 1 a useful means of measuring a pupil's progress. Once pupils are able to swim a minimum of 5 metres, they will be eligible to attempt the Distance Awards, details of which appear in Appendix 2.

3 • Activities and Games for Non-swimmers and Beginners

It is important to appreciate that non-swimmers have adjustments to make during visits to the swimming pool, especially in the early stages of getting used to the water. First of all there is the difference in temperature between the body and the water. Then there is the density of the water which has to be appreciated and the realisation that moving through water is quite different from moving on land where air pressure offers negligible resistance. The pressure of the water on the body, and particularly on the chest, can also make breathing more of a conscious effort. Furthermore, the possible fear of submersion and the discomfort of having water splashed on the face can often inhibit movement and bring about a reluctance to leave the poolside.

To help non-swimmers to adjust to movement in water, it is necessary to provide a programme of confidence-building activities in which the main aim is to dispel anxiety.

In an organised situation, such as a swimming lesson, pupils are likely to be distracted from any inhibiting factors if they are presented with play-like activities which they find both interesting and enjoyable.

It is recommended that a variety of buoyancy aids are available so that the teachers can decide which type or combination will be most appropriate for each pupil's needs or for the activity to be performed. The most commonly used aids are inflatable arm bands, inflatable rings and floats. It is important to remember that the aids should be close-fitting and there should be no possibility of them slipping off.

INTRODUCTION TO THE WATER

At the swimming pool pupils can have fun at the start by sitting on the edge of the pool, dangling their feet in the water and making a splash. Entries can then be made by carefully climbing down the steps, always facing the poolside. Once in the water further movement can be made, by stepping sideways close to the wall while holding the rail or trough, followed by sinking and rising movements to such descriptions as 'bobbing' or 'jack-in-the-box'. The more venturesome and confident pupils will no doubt create their own movements, perhaps moving away from the wall, turning around and 'washing themselves in the water'.

Entries may also be made by sitting on the poolside, turning sideways to place one hand across the body onto the poolside, then taking the weight on both hands and dropping into the water. As confidence is gained and when pupils have become accustomed to balancing themselves in the water, entries can be made by stepping from the poolside, with a partner in the water ready to assist and offer support if necessary. Further progression can be made by jumping into the water from a crouched position and then from a standing position. Once confidence has been developed through these methods of entry, further play-like activity can be introduced by encouraging pupils to enter the water with turns and shapes in the air, a reinforcement of activity that they will probably have already experienced in Physical Education lessons in school. Detailed descriptions of the various feet-first entries are to be found in Chapter 6.

MOVEMENT IN THE WATER

Once in the water, pupils should be encouraged to keep moving, ensuring where possible that their shoulders are below the surface so that the all-round support of the water can be felt. It is also warmer this way. For greater stability they should keep their feet apart and should hold their arms in outspread positions, pressing on the water to assist balance. Using a free formation and encouraging pupils to find a place by themselves will help to develop self-reliance.

In the sections that follow, play-like activities are suggested which will encourage non-swimmers and beginners to adjust to being in water, to lead them first to become waterborne and later to move into prone and supine positions, the prerequisites for more efficient movement through the water.

Although an effort has been made to present these activities in a logical sequence under appropriate headings, it should be appreciated that some of them do, in fact, fall into more than one category, e.g. in **Basking**

whales (see page 9), both submersion and breathing are involved. However, it is hoped that the classifications used will be helpful when considering which activities are most appropriate to the needs of the pupils being taught. It is suggested that teachers should adapt or modify the material to suit their pupils and the pool conditions. With careful selection by a sympathetic and enthusiastic teacher, not only should the pupils find the games and activities enjoyable but they should also gain in confidence and progress well.

For ease of reference, any starting positions are given first in brackets. These are followed by descriptions.

INDIVIDUAL ACTIVITIES AND GAMES

Activities to assist balance and movement in water

Bobbing
(Standing comfortably, facing the pool wall and holding the rail or trough with both hands.) Rise and sink gently and continuously, with the shoulders submerging. Progress to standing sideways with a single hand hold and, as confidence grows, move to a free standing position.

Making waves
- (Standing comfortably astride, feet close to the pool wall, holding the rail or trough with both hands.) By pushing backwards and forwards continuously, make waves with the back and chest.
- (Free standing, shoulders at the water surface.) Make waves by sweeping the arms sideways and forwards, with the palms leading.

Fig. 3: Crab walk

Crab walk *(see fig. 3)*
(Pupils stand spaced out in shallow water along the edges of the pool.) On the signal to begin, they grasp the rail or trough, lift their feet off the bottom and start walking crab-like along the sides of the pool, changing direction on the signal 'Move Right!' or 'Move Left!'.

Skiing
(Standing in free formation, shoulders submerged.) By sliding one foot after the other along the floor of the pool and using the arms for balance, movement away from the poolside can be made in a manner similar to walking on skis. Pressing backwards against the water with the arms will assist forward movement.

Duck walk
(Free standing, knees bent, shoulders submerged.) Keeping the chin at the water surface, walk like a duck, raising the feet slightly from the pool floor. Pull with the arms just below the surface to assist forward movement and make appropriate sounds by blowing into the water.

Frog jumps
(Free standing.) Pupils begin with their feet slightly astride and turned outwards, knees bent, shoulders in the water. They then travel forwards in small jumps, with their arms pulling sideways to assist propulsion and balance.

Marking time
(Free formation, shoulders submerged.) March slowly on the spot with high knee-raising and attempt to touch the forehead with each knee in turn. Spread the arms out to assist balance.

Fig. 4: Motor boats

Motor boats *(see fig. 4)*
(Free standing, with a float held out in front.) Using the float as a steering wheel, walk freely in different directions. Imitate the sound of a motor boat by blowing vigorously into the water.

Forming letters and figures
(Free standing, shoulders submerged.) Walk in various directions and, as the teacher calls out letters or numbers, stop and trace the shapes of these on the surface.

Miming
(Free standing.) As the teacher calls out words in some way associated with water – e.g. buoys, ducks, seagulls – the group attempts to perform an appropriate mime.

Follow the ball
(Standing in free formation, well apart.) Throw a ball, or suitable floating object, a short distance away, follow it, retrieve it and continue until told to stop.

Fig. 5: Chest ball

Chest ball (see fig. 5)
(Free formation.) Moving around the shallow area of the pool, attempt to propel a ball or other appropriate floating object by pushing it with the chest. This activity can be made competitive by pupils covering a set distance, or it could be used in relay form.

Hoop walk
(Free formation, holding a hoop.) With the hoop held on the water surface, discover different ways of walking, e.g. inside, outside, around. Later find other interesting ways of moving with the hoop.

Breathing practices

Blowing bubbles (1)
(Free standing.) Scoop up as much water as possible in cupped hands and then blow it away vigorously.

Blowing bubbles (2)
(Free standing, feet astride, hands on knees.) Lower the face into the water and blow bubbles:

- slowly – see who can make the longest blow
- suddenly – see who can make the loudest sound
- imaginatively – try to make different animal noises.

Drawing on the water
(Standing, one foot forwards.) Lean well forwards and, with the arms pressing firmly on the water to assist balance, use the nose to draw patterns or shapes on the water surface.

Blowing objects
(Free standing, water at shoulder level.) Walk around freely while blowing a light floating object, such as a cork or table tennis ball, along the water surface. Later this can be developed into a competitive activity over set distances.

Feed the ducks
(Free standing, shoulders submerged, chin at water level.) Walk freely, imitating the movements of a duck, with hands by the hips pushing backwards to assist propulsion. On the command 'Feed!', submerge the head momentarily, recover and carry on.

Basking whales
(Standing comfortably, feet slightly astride.) Inhale and hold the breath, then:
- submerge and breathe out slowly through the nose and mouth, watching the bubbles rise
- submerge and blow out explosively, like a whale.

Roll call
(Free standing, shoulders submerged.) Take a good breath, then attempt to call out individual names with the face lowered into the water.

Submersion practices

Dirty faces

(Standing comfortably near the poolside initially.) Scoop two handfuls of water and wash the face vigorously, as if it were really dirty. This activity can be modified by pouring water over the head and watching the water trickling down, thus encouraging the pupils to keep their eyes open. Furthermore, it encourages timid pupils to release their hold on the rail or trough.

Showers

(Free standing.) Scoop up as much water as possible in cupped hands, pour it from well above the head and watch it shower over the face and body. As an alternative, use a sponge, soak it thoroughly and squeeze it over the head. This activity can be performed in pairs, with each person taking it in turns to pour the water or to squeeze a sponge.

Fig. 6: Bobbing in twos

Bobbing in twos (see fig. 6)

(Standing facing a partner and holding each other's wrists.) After taking a breath, one partner bends his knees to submerge, and blows out through the mouth and nose. On returning to the surface for a breath, the other partner submerges and exhales. Pupils should try to develop a rhythmic action.

Fig. 7: Counting fingers

Counting fingers (see fig. 7)

(Standing, facing a partner.) After taking a breath, both crouch down to submerge, each counting the number of fingers displayed by the other. This activity encourages pupils to keep their eyes open underwater. It can be modified by asking them to take turns to make shapes with their hands when below the surface for their partners to identify.

Counting tiles

(Standing, facing the poolside.) Take a good breath and, starting at water level, touch and count each row of tiles, endeavouring to reach as far down as the pool floor. As a variation, stand with the face in the water and count the tiles immediately surrounding the feet, turning round to do so.

Catching the plate (1)

(Free standing, well spaced out.) Each pupil is provided with an object which will sink slowly, e.g. an enamel plate or a diving disc. This is released and when it begins to sink the pupil bobs down and tries to retrieve it. As confidence in submerging grows, pupils can practise leaving increasing intervals between release and submersion, so that the object is almost on the pool floor when retrieved.

Tall and small

(Free standing.) First reach upwards to go as high as possible, then sink by bending the knees and lowering the arms to submerge into a small, crouched position. Continue the movement rhythmically, with regular breathing added.

Sit down, reach up, turn round

(Free standing.) Attempt to sit on the bottom of the pool, stand and reach up high with the arms, then turn round.

Fig. 8: Jack-in-the-box

Jack-in-the-box (see fig. 8)

(Free standing.) Start off by 'bobbing' and gradually increase the range of movement until the head is completely submerged on the downward movement. The upward movement should be assisted by a jump to spring up as far as possible out of the water.

Show the knees

(Free standing.) This is a variation of Jack-in-the-box (above) and requires a vigorous upward jump to move the body high enough for the knees to rise above the water surface.

Attempt to maintain an erect body position throughout by keeping the head upright. (At a later stage this experience will prove helpful when feet-first entries are being practised from the poolside.)

Head, shoulders, knees and toes

(Free standing.) Using both hands, touch the head, shoulders, knees and toes, taking a good breath before submerging. This action can be accompanied by the instruction being chanted out rhythmically.

Buoyancy activities

Cycling (see fig. 9)

(Standing, shoulders submerged.) Holding a float under each arm, start by marking time (see page 8). Gradually develop a cycling action with the legs so that the feet no longer touch the bottom of the pool. Later, different types of leg movements may be tried to discover which is most effective in maintaining a supported, upright position.

Fig. 9: Cycling

Floating shapes

(Standing, shoulders submerged, holding a float under each arm.) Having experienced the buoyancy of the water, with both feet raised from the floor of the pool, discover ways of making different body shapes, e.g. tuck the knees to the chest, or extend the legs to make a long shape, prone or supine, with arms supported sideways on the floats. In the early stages this activity may be performed with a partner standing by to give support if required.

Gliding
In the early stages of learning to swim, discovering how to glide can be good fun. It can be performed in various ways.
- (Standing, shoulders submerged, arms forwards holding a float.) Raise one leg backwards, lean forwards slowly to lose balance and move into a glide. Keep the arms straight and hold the float firmly.
- (Starting position as above.) Face the poolside from a few metres away and push away from the pool floor to glide to the wall.
- (Starting position as before, but with the back to the poolside.) Place one foot against the wall and push away into a glide. Try to increase the distance each time an attempt is made. Later compete with others to see who can glide the furthest distance. Emphasis should be placed on taking a good breath before pushing off.
- Gliding can also be performed on the back, holding a float under each arm or a single float across the chest. As confidence grows, floats can be discarded and the pupils encouraged to attempt making various shapes while floating, e.g. long, wide, narrow, star-shaped, etc.

Sky diving
(Standing, shoulders submerged, arms forwards and well apart.) Raise one leg backwards, lean forwards to lose balance and move into a glide with legs apart, to take up a star-shape in the prone floating position.

Fig. 10: Mushroom float

Mushroom float *(see fig. 10)*
(Standing, shoulders submerged.) Take a full breath, put the face in the water, tuck the knees to the chest and clasp the arms around the lower legs. This will cause the body to rotate forwards with the back rounded (like the top of a mushroom) just above the surface of the water. To recover to a standing position, lift the head, causing the body to rotate upwards, push the feet towards the bottom of the pool and press downwards and sideways with the arms to assist balance.

CLASS ACTIVITIES AND GAMES

Although in the following activities and games pupils will be involved collectively, it should be appreciated that the response of the pupils themselves will still remain very much at a personal level.

Having become accustomed to the water, they are now afforded opportunities of extending their experience in a wider context. More specific groupings in games relationships will be presented later in this chapter.

Free and caught
A catcher is chosen and is given an arm band to wear. Another player wears two bands. The remaining players move about freely until tagged by the player with the one arm band, at which point they must remain where they are, bobbing up and down. However, when touched by the player with two arm bands

they become free again. Frequent changes of those wearing arm bands will maintain interest and add variety to this game.

Simon says

Standing and well spaced apart, the pupils imitate the teacher's commands or actions, but only if they are preceded by the words 'Simon says'. To avoid elimination and consequent inactivity for moving at the wrong time, each pupil starts with 10 points, losing one point for each mistake.

Here, there, where

The pupils are freely spaced, standing with shoulders at water level. As the teacher calls out 'Here!', the pupils move to the right, on the word 'There!', they move to the left, and on 'Where!', they remain in place, bobbing up and down. This game may also be played by the pupils following the direction indicated by the teacher's thumb.

All-in tag

All the players carry an arm band and are free except the one who is 'It', who *wears* an arm band. When touched, a player must put on the arm band and join the other catchers in tagging the ones who are still free. The game continues until only one free player remains.

Touches

A number of floating objects are scattered in the shallow end of the pool – e.g. balls, arm bands – and other objects are set out on the sides of the pool. As the teacher names an object or the colour of an object, the players attempt to touch it.

Ship's salvage

Floating objects, such as corks, arm bands, balls, etc., are arranged along the centre of the pool. Starting in the water at the poolside, pupils move forwards and attempt to collect as many items as possible, but only one at a time, placing them on the poolside for a final count.

Treasure hunt

This game is similar to **Ship's salvage** (see above), but suitable sinkable objects are included. Points can be awarded for the objects retrieved, e.g. floating objects – 1 point; sinkable objects – 2 points; small sinkable objects – 3 points.

Sly shark

The players are arranged on opposite sides of the pool, facing across. One or two players, chosen to be the 'sharks', stand in the middle, with only heads above the water, quietly blowing bubbles. Players then attempt to cross to the opposite side of the pool. Suddenly, on a known signal, the 'sharks' give chase while the other players try to gain the safety of the nearest side of the pool. Any pupils who are caught change places with the 'sharks' who have caught them. The number of 'sharks' will be determined by the size of the group taking part.

Simple tag

All the players are spaced out freely, except for the one chosen to be the catcher, who stands some distance away facing them. When the signal to start is given, the catcher tries to tag one of the players. If 'tagged', a player takes the place of the catcher.

Floating tag

This form of tag can be played once pupils are waterborne. Players cannot be 'tagged' if they are floating or if they have both feet off the floor of the pool.

Red letter

The pupils stand with their backs to the poolside. The teacher, on the opposite side, calls out letters at random. If the letter called appears anywhere in a player's name, that player is allowed to take a step forwards. Whenever the teacher calls out a previously designated 'red letter', no one must move. Anyone caught out must take a step backwards. The aim of this game is to see who is first to cross the pool.

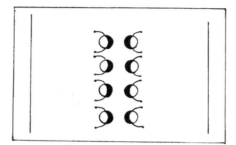

Fig. 11: Crusts and crumbs

Crusts and crumbs *(see fig. 11)*

The pupils stand in two files in the centre of the pool, back to back and about a metre apart. One line is designated 'Crusts' and the other, 'Crumbs'. If the teacher calls out 'Crusts!', the pupils in that line attempt to reach their side of the pool before the others can turn round and tag them, and vice versa. To keep the pupils alert, the teacher may prolong the first syllable before adding the second, e.g. 'Crrrr . . . usts!' or 'Crrrr . . . umbs!' Occasionally variations such as 'Crrrr . . . ackers!' or 'Crrrr . . . umpet!' may be introduced to add a little spice to the game. To make it competitive, each team may keep a score of the numbers tagged.

Supermarket

A selection of floating objects is scattered in the centre of the pool. Starting from the pool-side and using a floatboard as a shopping trolley, each player attempts to collect as many objects as possible. After a set time, or when all the objects have been collected, the player with the most objects on the float-board is the winner.

Sly fox

The teacher stands on the poolside, with his back to the pupils who stand at the opposite side of the pool facing across. When the signal to start is given, the pupils begin to walk slowly and quietly towards the opposite side. Whenever the teacher calls out 'Fox!', turning round as he does so, anyone caught moving has to take two steps backwards. The game proceeds, with the teacher repeating this at frequent intervals. The game is over when the first pupil succeeds in reaching the teacher's side of the pool and calls out 'Safe!'.

Red rover

One pupil is chosen to be the caller and stands in the middle of the pool. The other players are at one side of the pool facing the caller. The poolside behind the caller is the 'Caller's den'. When the caller says 'Red rover, Red rover, send . . . over', naming one of the players, that player must try to reach 'Caller's den' without being tagged by the caller. If successful, the player returns to the starting side. If caught, the player must stay in 'Caller's den'. The caller can call for more than one person at a time, or say 'Red rover, Red rover, send everyone over'. In this case all the players try to reach the opposite side without being caught. The caller should be changed from time to time. The caller who ends up with the most players in 'Caller's den' becomes the winner.

Pass the water *(see fig. 12)*

Pupils form a circle in chest deep water, turning left so that they are facing the back of

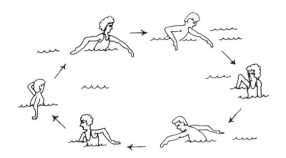

Fig. 12: Pass the water

the person in front. On a given signal, they start to walk in a clockwise direction, 'passing' the water in front of them to the person behind them by using a crawl stroke pull that ends above the surface.

Washing machine

Groups of six pupils or more hold hands in a circle in chest deep water. When the teacher calls out 'Washer on!', the pupils sway from side to side in unison to make a swishing noise. When the teacher calls out 'Soap!', they bob up and down, blowing bubbles as they submerge briefly, to simulate the addition of soap powder to the wash. Finally, on the command 'Spin!', they start to run round in a circle as if spinning the clothes. When the water is moving fast, the teacher calls out 'Switch off!', and the pupils stop.

Green light, red light

This is suitable for groups of six and upwards, in water up to chest depth. One pupil, who stands at the finishing line on one side of the pool, becomes 'It'. At the start of the game, he turns so that his back is towards the rest of the group. 'It' starts the game by calling out 'Green!', and the others try to make their way to the finishing line. When 'It' calls out 'Red!' and turns round, all players must stay where they are. If 'It' catches any players moving,

they must return to the starting line. The first person to reach the finishing line is the winner and becomes 'It' in the next game.

Fill the Space

In chest deep water and in groups of six or more, the pupils stand in a circle and each is given an appropriate name, e.g. whales, dolphins, seals etc. One pupil, who stands in the middle, becomes 'It'. When 'It' calls out one of the names, e.g. 'Seals!', everyone who is a seal changes places with another seal. While this is happening, 'It' tries to fill one of the empty spaces around the circle.

The person who is left without a place becomes the new 'It'.

ACTIVITIES AND GAMES WITH A PARTNER

Having been involved in a variety of individual water activities, pupils should now have gained sufficient self-confidence to relate more closely with others: first with a partner, then with groups of three or more in co-operative or competitive situations.

Finding a partner

Rather than choosing the nearest person, a fun way of finding a partner is for each pupil to move around calling out his initials until another pupil with one of the same initials is found. For example, a pupil with the initials J. M. B. can pair up with someone with the initials B. S. or D. B. T.

Dodging in pairs

One partner chases the other until the teacher calls out 'Stop!' If the one who is chasing can reach out and touch his partner without taking a step forwards, a point is gained. The roles are then changed and the game continues.

Two dogs and a bone

Two players stand opposite each other in mid-pool, about four metres apart, with a small floating object – e.g. a quoit, arm band, ball or cork – halfway between them. On a signal each attempts to grasp the object to take it back to the nearest side without being tagged. Lines on the pool floor or markers on the poolside can be used to distance the players.

Coupled race

The class is arranged in pairs, who stand with their backs to the poolside, each with the inner arm around the waist of the other. On a signal each pair attempts to be first to cross the pool without breaking the grasp. The free arms can be used to assist balance and to provide propulsion.

Count the passes

Pupils stand in pairs a few metres apart, each pair with a ball or quoit. Following a brief practice in throwing and catching, each pair tries to make as many consecutive passes as possible in a given time. A missed catch means that the pair involved must restart counting.

See-saw *(see fig. 13)*

Partners stand facing each other, with shoulders beneath the water and holding hands. One partner rises by stretching upwards, while the other sinks below the surface by bending the knees. Positions are then changed and the action is continued. Before submerging a good breath should be taken and pupils encouraged to breathe out, trickle fashion, whilst submerged.

Sawing wood

Pupils start by facing each other with shoulders submerged, feet slightly apart, one foot forwards and the other foot back. From

Fig. 13: See-saw

this position, each bends the forward knee and reaches forwards to grasp the other's hands. They then move the arms forwards and backwards with a full stretch, miming the action of sawing wood. (This experience can be useful when pupils need to reach forwards with their arms when performing dog paddle.)

Catching the plate (2)

This is a variation of **Catching the plate (1)** (see page 10). One partner has an object, such as a diving disc or quoit, which will sink slowly. This is released for the other one to try to retrieve before it reaches the bottom. Later, the object can be allowed to reach the bottom of the pool and, standing some distance apart, both of them can submerge to retrieve it. The first to surface with the object scores a point and a competition can be held to see which one reaches a given number of points first.

Couple tag

Two players with inner hands joined are chosen to be the catchers in this game. As they tag other players, they in turn join the line until there are four catchers. Two then break off to form a separate pair of catchers. The game proceeds in the same way until there are no free players. This may be played in free

Fig. 14: Over and under passing

formation or across the pool, with the catchers situated in the middle.

Twin tag

The players are arranged in pairs, one player standing close behind his partner, grasping his hips. All players remain in similar contact and the game proceeds as in **Simple tag** (see page 12), with the couple chosen to be chasers trying to tag another couple who then become the taggers instead.

Through the hoop

Each player takes turns to hold a hoop for his partner to move through. The hoop may be held vertically or horizontally, on or below the surface. Partners may also move simultaneously or in succession, both holding the hoop. Pupils should be encouraged to devise their own movements and sequences.

Over and under passing (see fig. 14)

Each pair stand back to back, with feet astride. A ball, quoit or other suitable object is passed from one to the other, first back over the head and then down between the legs. This activity can be made competitive by seeing which pair is first to complete a given number of passes.

One leg balance (see fig. 15)

Partners face each other a short distance apart, with arms stretched forwards. They then raise one leg backwards and attempt to balance on the other, so that the body is in a near horizontal position at water level. Later, when complete confidence has been gained, this activity can be made competitive, with one partner trying to unbalance the other, using only gentle hand pressure.

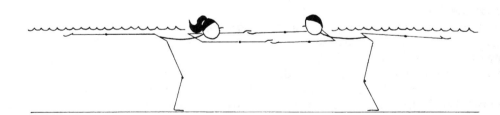

Fig. 15: One leg balance

Towing in pairs *(see figs 16a, b and c)*

This activity may be performed in the following ways:

- Standing one behind the other, with shoulders at water level. The rear partner holds the hips or shoulders of the one in front, who travels forwards using the arms to assist balance and propulsion.
- Standing facing each other, shoulders at water level, each using a forearm grasp. One walks backwards, towing the other in a horizontal, prone position.
- Standing one behind the other, with shoulders at water level. The rear partner places the hands under the shoulders of the one in front, who takes up a supine, horizontal position. The rear partner tows by walking backwards.

In each activity the one who is being towed may use the legs to maintain a horizontal position and to provide some propulsion. They may be used competitively over short distances, with partners changing places at the halfway stage.

Partner tag

All players are arranged in pairs, with one from each couple being chosen to be the chaser. When tagged, the roles are reversed and the game continues.

Wheelbarrows *(see fig. 17)*

One partner takes up a prone or supine position, with legs apart, and the other stands between the legs and supports at the hips. The 'wheelbarrow' may glide with arms extended beyond the head or use the arms for balance and propulsion. With confident pupils this may be developed into a competitive activity, over short distances, with partners changing places halfway through the race.

Fig. 16a

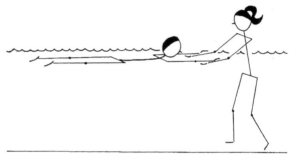

Fig. 16b

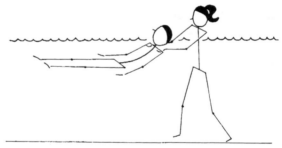

Fig. 16c

Bouncing ball *(see fig. 18)*

Partners stand facing each other. One, the 'ball', stands with arms by the sides of the body. The other, the 'bouncer', places one hand lightly on the 'ball's' head. The 'ball' now starts to spring up and down like a bouncing ball. The jumps can be assisted by the 'bouncer' supporting lightly with hands on each side of the partner's chest.

Fig. 17: Wheelbarrows (supine position, above left; prone position, above right)

Fig. 18: Bouncing ball

Fig. 19: One against two

GROUP ACTIVITIES AND GAMES

Forming groups

The pupils stand freely spaced in the water at the start of this activity. When the teacher calls out a number, preferably between 1 and 6, pupils form groups of that number. This is a fun way of forming groups for subsequent games.

One against two (see fig. 19)

The players are arranged in threes. Two in each group take up a position whereby one stands behind the other, with hands on the hips of the person in front. The third player, who stands facing them, attempts to touch

the player at the rear, while the other two move around trying to prevent this. The front player is allowed to spread his arms out sideways to act as a barrier, but he must not hold or push the catcher.

Towing in threes

The pupils are in threes, standing abreast. Those on the outside who act as supporters place their inner hand firmly on their hip, with the outer arm ready for support and propulsion. The middle one takes up a supine or prone floating position and, grasping the forearms of the supporters, is towed across the pool. After initial practices, this can be made into a competitive activity, with players taking it in turns to be towed across.

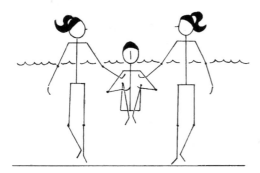

Fig. 20: Carrying the bucket

Carrying the bucket (see fig. 20)

This is similar to **Towing in threes** (see previous page), but instead of being towed across the pool, the middle pupil is carried. The two supporters grasp the middle person under the arms. The one in the middle takes up a tucked position, with arms clasped around his lower legs, and is carried across the width of the pool. Like **Towing in threes**, this can be used as a competitive game, with players being carried in turn.

Chain tag

This game is started with two players being chosen as catchers. They then stand side by side, with hands joined and in the middle of the group. As players are caught, they join up to form a long chain until only one remains. This game, too, can be a competitive one, by starting with two or three pairs of catchers who try to form the longest chain.

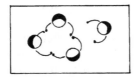

Fig. 21: One against three

One against three (see fig. 21)

Three players join hands to form a circle, facing inwards. A fourth player, moving around the circle, attempts to touch a nominated member of the circle while the others dodge about to avoid this. The roles of the players should be changed frequently to maintain interest. The winner is the one who makes the biggest number of touches.

Fig. 22: Fox and geese

Fox and geese (see fig. 22)

Three or four players, the 'geese', form a line, one behind the other, each grasping firmly the hips of the one in front. Another player, the 'fox', attempts to catch the one at the rear by moving around and changing direction quickly, while the rest weave and dodge without breaking their grasp. If successful, the 'fox' joins the 'geese' and goes to the back of the line, while the front player becomes the 'fox'.

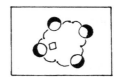

Fig. 23: Poison

Poison (see fig. 23)

The players join hands in a circle, facing inwards. A floating object, such as a large ball, float or rubber ring, is placed in the middle. The players then attempt to pull each other in such a way that someone touches the object. The person who has been 'poisoned' the least number of times during the game is the winner. Groups should be small, e.g. 4–6 players, so that there is ample activity for all in the class.

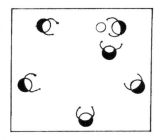

Fig. 24: Wandering ball

Wandering ball (1) *(see fig. 24)*

In this game the players form a circle, facing inwards and well spread out. One player is chosen to be in the middle. A ball is passed across or around the circle, with the middle player attempting to intercept. If successful, he changes place with the thrower. In the interests of fair play, the ball must not be thrown above reachable height. If desired, the game can be played with more than one player in the middle. (In deep water, with the players swimming or treading water, this game can provide useful practice for water polo.)

Circle chase

A large circle of six to eight players is formed, with the players facing inwards and in twos. On a signal, 'odds' or 'evens' travel around the circle in a stated direction, attempting to be first back in place.

Horses and jockeys (1) *(see fig. 25)*

The players form two concentric circles facing inwards, each player in the outer circle having a partner of a similar size. On a signal to start, those on the outside travel round the circle in a clockwise direction, returning to mount

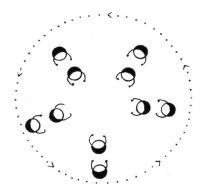

Fig. 25: Horses and jockeys (1)

their partners' backs. The first 'jockey' back in position, astride his partner's back, is the winner. After each circuit the players change places. This game can be varied by starting from a mounted position, or by the 'jockeys' first going between the 'horses'' legs (held in a wide astride position) before travelling round the circle.

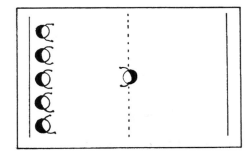

Fig. 26: Chinese line (1)

Chinese line (1) *(see fig. 26)*

The players start at one side of the pool facing the other side. Those chosen to act as catchers – usually two or three to begin with – stand in a line down the centre of the pool facing them. When the game starts, the players attempt to cross the pool without being tagged. Those who are tagged join in a line with the catchers. The last player to remain 'free' is the winner. The catchers may only move sideways and must not stray from a line down the middle of the pool. This can be indicated by markers on the poolside at each end or by using the markings on the pool floor. A variation of the game is for those who are caught to change places with the catcher.

Follow the leader (1)

In small groups and well spaced out, the players follow the actions of their leaders, who may travel in various directions or perform actions on the spot. To maintain interest, there should be frequent changes of leaders.

Fig. 27: Rocking the dummy

Rocking the dummy (see fig. 27)

Two supporting players stand about double-arm distance apart, in a stable, lunge position, with a third player standing in between, holding himself rigid, arms at the sides. The middle player tilts forwards or backwards and is then gently rocked between the two supporters.

Guarding the hoop (see fig. 28)

One player chosen to act as a guard stands with his back to a floating hoop. The remainder

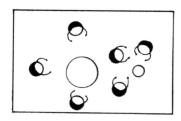

Fig. 28: Guarding the hoop

of the group (4–6 players) are some two metres away in circle formation. When play begins, the players try to throw a ball so that it lands in the hoop guarded by the centre player. A successful thrower changes places with the guard. Players should be encouraged to pass the ball quickly from one to the other to get the centre player off guard before aiming at the hoop.

Pass ball

Small teams of players face each other from opposite sides of the pool. A large ball is thrown into the centre of the pool and each side attempts to gain possession. The ball is passed from one player to another to score by touching it against the opponent's side of the pool. After a goal is scored, a player from the other side throws the ball into the middle of the pool and the game proceeds. Instead of using the sides of the pool, floating hoops may be used as goal targets and these can be arranged to modify the distances to be covered.

Ball tag

This game is played like **Simple tag** (see page 13), but the method of tagging is by hitting a player with a soft ball (such as a beach ball), which is thrown by the one chosen to be the tagger. As before, if a player is tagged, he takes the place of the thrower.

Overhead passing relay

The players stand in line, in teams of four, one behind the other and about one metre apart. The front player in each team passes a ball or other suitable object overhead to the next player behind and so on to the end of the team. The last player, still holding the ball, moves to the front of the team and the play continues until the original leader has returned to the front and is holding the ball overhead. As a variation, the ball may be passed sideways down the line.

Over and under relay

This game is similar to the **Overhead passing relay** (see above) except that the ball, or other object, is passed down the line over the head and between the legs, until it reaches the last player who moves to the front . . . and so on.

Keep the ball up

Small groups, each with a large ball, attempt to make as many consecutive passes as possible in a given time. If a ball is dropped, counting must be restarted from the beginning.

Merry-go-round

An even number of pupils are arranged in a circle, facing inwards and numbered in twos. No. 1s remain standing with hands firmly on their hips. No. 2s, while grasping the forearms of the supporters on each side, take up a back floating position, with their feet towards the centre of the circle. When all are settled in position, the supporters step sideways, in unison, either clockwise or anticlockwise. The floaters may perform a gentle flutter with their legs to help maintain a horizontal position. The situation is then reversed, with no. 2s acting as supporters. As a variation, this activity may be performed with a light ball at the feet of the floaters, who attempt to pass it around the circle in the opposite direction to that of travel.

Dodge ball (1)

The players form a circle and one player is chosen to go into the middle. Using a soft ball, the players then try to hit the person in the middle. Any player making a hit becomes the target, and the game continues.

Dodge ball (2)

In this version there are two players in the circle, one behind and holding the hips of the other. The object of the game is to attempt to hit the rear player with the ball. This encourages the players in the circle to pass the ball to someone more favourably placed to try to make the hit.

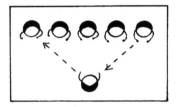

Fig. 29: Corner spry (1)

Corner spry (1) (see fig. 29)

Each of the teams is arranged in a line facing one player with a ball. The ball is thrown and returned by each player in turn down the line. When the last player receives the ball, he takes the place of the thrower who joins the line as number one. The play continues until all players have returned to their original places. The first team to do so wins the game.

'Potato' race (see fig. 30)

A small number of floating objects are set out in line across the pool Starting from the poolside, competitors collect the objects, carrying them one at a time, and place them on the poolside. The winner is the first to collect all the objects set out for him.

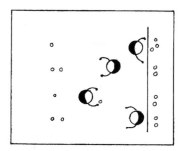

Fig. 30: 'Potato' race

Newcombe (1) *(see fig. 31)*

In this game the teams take up position on each side of a rope or net suspended across the middle of the playing area. The object of the game is to throw a ball over the net so that it falls on the water in the opponents' court. The game is started by a server throwing the ball from the rear of the court over the rope. This may be done directly or by passing the ball to other players on the same side who may not drop the ball before it passes over the rope. No more than three passes may be made by any team at any time and the ball may be held only momentarily. It may be pushed or volleyed with the palms of the hands but it may not be punched. One team continues to serve until a point is lost, when the other team takes over. At each change of service, players move one place around. A point is scored if the ball alights on the water in the opponents' court and the first team to score a given number of points wins the game.

Empty the hoop

The players are arranged in small groups, each of which has a floating hoop containing a specific number of buoyant objects. One group plays against another and attempts to empty its own hoop by carrying and placing the objects, one at a time, into the opposing team's hoop. When the game is halted, the group with the least number of objects remaining is the winner.

Target ball *(see fig. 32)*

This is a ball-passing game played across the pool by two teams. Suitable goals are placed at each end of the playing area. Piles of floats, skittles or hoops fixed in stands might be used for this purpose. Each team starts from its own side of the pool and attempts to be first to retrieve a ball thrown into the middle. The object of the game is to pass and throw the ball through the opponents' goal. A player is allowed only three steps before passing to another player and at least three passes must be made before an attempt can be made to score. Physical contact is not permitted, but

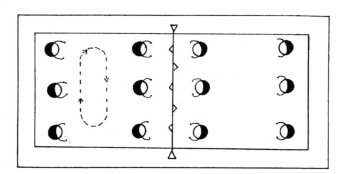

Fig. 31: Newcombe

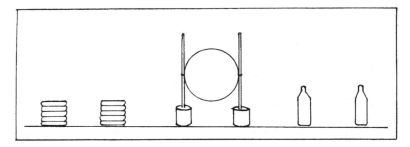

Fig. 32: Target ball

close marking should be encouraged. After each goal the game is restarted by possession of the ball being given to the team against which the goal was scored.

Scatter dodge ball (1)

The players form a circle and each is given a number. A soft ball is thrown into the centre of the circle and when the teacher calls out a number, that particular player moves forwards to collect the ball while the others scatter. As soon as the ball has been collected, the one in possession calls out 'Stop!' and all must do so and remain still, with arms stretched sideways out of the water. He then attempts to hit someone with the ball, scoring a point if he succeeds. The game continues by the players re-forming a circle and the teacher throwing the ball into the centre and calling out another number.

Cat and mouse

The players stand in a circle facing inwards and looking downwards. The player chosen to be the 'mouse' walks round the circle quietly and touches one of the players on the shoulder. This player then becomes the 'cat' and chases the 'mouse' around the circle. If the 'mouse' returns to take the empty space before being touched, the 'cat' takes his place as the 'mouse'. If not, another 'mouse' is chosen.

Squirrel and nut

This game is similar to **Cat and mouse** (see above) except that a player is chosen to be the 'squirrel' and walks round the circle carrying a small ball or other object to represent the 'nut'. Those in the circle look downwards, as before, but they hold their hands behind their backs, with fingers linked. The 'squirrel' walks round the circle and quietly drops the 'nut' into the cupped hands of one of the other players. The player who has received it chases the 'squirrel' round the circle and, again, the aim is to occupy the empty space without being touched. If this happens, the chaser takes the 'squirrel's' place and the game continues.

Broncho

The players form groups of three, standing one behind the other and grasping the waist of the one in front to form a 'broncho'. Another player is then chosen to be the catcher and he takes up a position one or two metres away from the 'broncho', facing the leader. When the game starts, the catcher tries to attach himself to the 'broncho' by catching hold of the last in the line around the waist. The 'broncho' tries to prevent him from doing so by twisting and turning. If the catcher succeeds, he changes places with the one at the front of the 'broncho'.

Twos and threes *(see fig. 33)*

The players are arranged in pairs, one behind the other in a circle formation. At the start of the game two players are chosen, one to chase the other. The one who is being chased can rest by standing either in front of or behind any of the couples in the circle. If he stands in front, the player at the back becomes the one to be chased. Should he stand behind, the front player is the one to be chased. When a player is tagged, he becomes the chaser. For maximum activity, this game should be played in small groups.

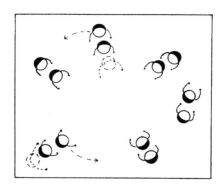

Fig. 33: Twos and threes

4 • Activities and Games for Swimmers

Once pupils can swim confidently, irrespective of specific style or technique, they should be ready to apply their newly acquired skills and to widen their experience.

Both at this stage and later, play activity and games can still be of great value as an enjoyable means of introducing pupils to more advanced skills. For the competitive swimmer they can provide a welcome and purposeful break from the strict routine of training. They can also provide a foundation for a whole range of water activities to be pursued for their own intrinsic values and purposes.

However, it is important to appreciate that involvement in play and games does not mean that pupils are left to their own devices, nor should there be lack of endeavour. Careful guidance is still required so that greater satisfaction can be gained from play and this means that revision of certain previously acquired skills will often be necessary.

Two invaluable and closely related skills which have important applications in all swimming activities are **sculling** and **treading water**. Accordingly, special mention is made of these skills, which are described below.

SCULLING

In its most usual form this is executed with the body in a horizontal, supine position in the water. From this position, and with the palms of the hands leading, the arms move slightly outwards and inwards, smoothly and continuously. In so doing, the hands are moved through a figure-of-eight pathway. Propulsion is caused by the pressure of the hands against the water. If the pressure is mainly downwards, the body is prevented from sinking and remains stationary. Pressure directed towards the feet will move the body head-first, and pressure in the opposite direction will cause the body to move feet-first. When sculling, the hands should remain naturally curved, with the fingers together.

Pressure is always applied in the opposite direction to the intended line of travel.

Many manoeuvres of the body through water are performed by sculling actions in a variety of forms, with the hands moving simultaneously, alternately, near to, and away from the body or in opposite directions to each other. Exploring the possibilities can be enjoyable and should be strongly encouraged, once the basic movements have been taught.

TREADING WATER

To maintain an upright position with the head above water, the feet are pressed downwards as if walking up a flight of stairs, thereby causing an upward reaction which prevents the body from sinking. Additional upthrust can be provided by sculling with the hands and forearms just wide and forward of the shoulders to exert downward pressure. In order to provide and to maintain upward thrust the legs may be used simultaneously as in breast stroke, alternately as in the crawl strokes, or spirally, with the legs moving like 'eggbeaters' (see fig. 98 on page 63). Like sculling, this activity can provide fun through discovering ways of changing direction, of aiming for height, making shapes and patterns with the arms out of the water, and of travelling.

INDIVIDUAL ACTIVITIES AND GAMES

Swim walk
The pupils start by treading water and then attempt to 'walk' in various directions while keeping their bodies upright. This may be developed into a competitive activity by seeing who can 'swim walk' across the pool first.

Porter race
Treading water and travelling forwards while holding a light object (e.g. an arm band or a float) out of the water or on the head, pupils attempt to be first to cross the pool.

Leaping salmon
While treading water, pupils thrust vigorously with their legs, assisted by downward pressure with their arms, to raise their bodies as high as possible out of the water. Progress can be made by reaching up with the arms.

Handstands
Starting from a standing position, with the arms raised and the head down, pupils spring into a surface dive to reach for the pool floor, to stand on their hands. Recovery is either by sinking to a crouch position and then standing or by bending the arms, allowing the legs to sink into an upward glide.

Hand walks
From a handstand position in the water, pupils attempt to walk in various directions and to turn around. In this activity and the preceding one, the arms should be bent to change level and explore other possibilities of movement in an inverted position. It is helpful, throughout, to feel the support of the water surrounding the body. Needless to say, a good breath and good breath-holding capacity are required. See also **Partner handstand** on page 41.

Fig. 34: Monkey up a stick

Monkey up a stick (see fig. 34)
From a standing position pupils spring upwards as high as possible, with their arms extended beyond their heads. Then they sink to a crouch position, place their hands on the bottom of the pool, invert their bodies and stretch their legs upwards and out of the water. These actions are performed continuously. If swimmers are very strong and proficient, this activity can be performed while treading water. A powerful kick is used to raise the body out of the water, followed by forward rotation on sinking, so that the body is inverted. A very powerful downward thrust is then made with the arms to raise the legs out of the water.

Fig. 35: Sculling head-first

Sculling head-first *(see fig. 35)*

Starting in a back floating position, with the arms straight and by the sides, the wrists are hyper-extended with the fingers pointing upwards. The hands now perform sculling actions, with pressure exerted towards the feet.

Fig. 36: Sculling feet-first

Sculling feet-first *(see fig. 36)*

From the same starting position as in **Sculling head-first** (see above), the wrists are then flexed with the fingers pointing downwards towards the bottom of the pool. Pressure is now exerted towards the head.

Fig. 37: Stationary scull

Stationary scull *(see fig. 37)*

In this form the wrists are straight, with fingers pointing towards the feet, and pressure is exerted downwards.

Washing tub

From a stationary sculling position, the knees are drawn up towards the chest so that the body assumes a tucked position. Each hand

then performs sculling actions, but in opposite directions. This causes the body to spin round. Frequent changes of speed and direction should be attempted to develop control. A variation is to perform rotations with the body fully extended, again sculling in opposite directions with the hands.

Water wheel

From a stationary sculling position the body is moved to a tucked position and then tilted to one side. The upper hand is placed on the hip, elbow pointing outwards. The lower arm performs a flat sculling action to maintain the body at the surface, while the legs perform a cycling action to cause the body to spin round. A small splash with the feet and lower legs is then added.

Spinning top

While treading water using an 'eggbeater' kick (see fig. 98 on page 63), the arms are held at the sides of the body with each hand sculling in opposite directions. These actions will cause the body to rotate vertically. Changes of speed, direction and level can then be attempted.

Fig. 38: Canoe

Canoe *(see fig. 38)*

The body is in a prone, horizontal position, with the back slightly arched so that the mouth is clear of the water and the heels are at the surface. The arms are extended alongside the body, with the hands close to the hips and the fingers pointing downwards. The hands now perform sculling actions, with pressure being directed towards the feet so that the body travels in a head-first direction.

Jelly fish

From the **Mushroom float** (see page 12), the limbs are gradually moved outwards to hang loosely, while the body remains floating. Recovery is either by treading water or by regaining a standing position.

Floating letters

From prone or supine floating positions the arms and legs are extended gradually and smoothly in different directions to form the shapes of letters, e.g. Y, K, X or I.

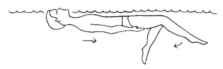

Fig. 39: Marching in the water

Marching in the water (see fig. 39)

While sculling feet-first (see page 29), introduce a walking action by gently dropping the lower legs and using them to exert strong backward pressure. The knees remain just below the surface. As progress is made, the hands may be placed on the hips so that propulsion is produced by the legs only.

Fewest strokes contest

While swimming breast stroke or elementary back stroke, the glide is prolonged so that the pupils endeavour to cover a given distance using the fewest number of strokes. This activity can also be performed by using only the leg actions of these strokes.

Pendulum (1) (see fig. 40)

From a back floating position and performing a stationary sculling action, the head is raised, the knees are tucked to the chest and the pupil rotates to a vertical position. Maintaining a sculling action, the head is then lowered forwards and the legs are extended backwards so that a front floating position is achieved. These actions are then reversed and are continued to create a pendulum-type movement.

Pendulum (2) (see fig. 41)

This is a variation of **Pendulum (1)** (see above), with the arms held sideways and the hands performing a flat sculling action to maintain balance. The head is raised forwards to allow the legs to sink slowly, until the body assumes a vertical position. A strong sculling action is maintained to support the body and to keep the head above water. The head is next lowered forwards and the legs are moved backwards and upwards so that the body adopts a prone floating position. The actions are then continued.

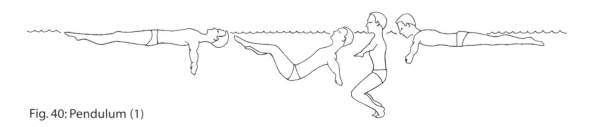

Fig. 40: Pendulum (1)

Fig. 41: Pendulum (2)

Fig. 42: Swimming like a crab

Fig. 43: Torpedo

Swimming like a crab

- Starting from a prone floating position, in the shape of a star, pupils attempt to swim sideways using alternating sculling-type actions with the legs and arms. Pressure should be exerted in the opposite direction to the intended line of travel.
- Starting from a prone floating position, with the arms extended forwards, pupils attempt to swim backwards by using reverse breast stroke action. This involves the arms for propulsion and using a flutter kick with the legs to prevent them from sinking.
- A variation of the above can be performed by keeping the arms extended and fairly close together, with the hands performing sculling movements (*see fig. 42*). The wrists

should be hyper-extended, with the fingers facing upwards, pressure being exerted away from the head, resulting in backward travel through the water.

Torpedo (see fig. 43)

This is performed in a supine position, with the arms extended beyond the head. With the wrists hyper-extended and with fingers pointing downwards, the hands perform a sculling action to propel the body feet-first. The hips should be held high and the toes should skim the water surface.

Rotation swimming (see fig. 44)

This is a combination of front and back crawl. The strokes are alternated by rotating the body on the recovery of each arm, so that

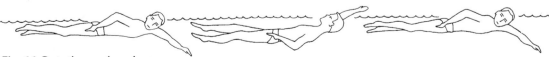

Fig. 44: Rotation swimming

the body is prone for one arm pull and supine for the next. It is important to maintain a smooth and continuous leg kick to keep the body extended and also to reach for the entry of each arm. In the early stages it is helpful to perform a few cycles of each stroke before rotating.

Fig. 45: Submarine

Submarine *(see fig. 45)*
While sculling in a head-first position, one knee is bent to raise the leg until it becomes perpendicular. By changing the position of the hands and exerting upward pressure, the body can be submerged to travel beneath the surface, with the lower part of the raised leg assuming the appearance of a submarine periscope. A flat sculling action with very strong downward pressure will be required to return to the surface and continue travelling.

Porpoise
This involves a series of shallow surface dives interspersed with very short underwater swims using breast stroke. Regular breaths can be taken as the head clears the surface. To travel up and over the surface requires a very strong pull with the arms and a powerful thrust of the legs.

Seal
This is a similar type of activity to the **Porpoise** (see above). However, a sculling action is used, with the arms at the sides of the body and the hands exerting backward pressure to effect movement through the water. Changes of direction can be made by turning the head and twisting the body. Occasional shallow surface dives can be added to simulate the movement of a seal.

Shark
Imitating a shark, pupils swim face downwards using both legs and one arm. The other arm is held with the palm of the hand placed sideways on top of the head, to represent the shark's triangular fin.

Football
While sculling feet-first, players attempt to propel a ball using only the feet. This activity can be made competitive over short distances.

Silent swimming contest
Each pupil attempts to cross the pool by making as little noise as possible and using either a nominated stroke or a free choice of strokes. This is a useful practice to encourage swimmers to concentrate on smooth, controlled actions. The best two or three may be chosen to demonstrate afterwards, with appropriate teaching points being made.

Duck dive
While swimming breast stroke, the arms are pulled back strongly, the head is dropped and the knees are brought forwards into a tucked position. This will then cause the body to rotate into a vertical position from which it can sink into a dive as the legs are extended. This is a useful preliminary practice for the head-first surface dive or a forward somersault.

Fig.46: Surface diving, head-first

Surface diving, head-first *(see fig. 46)*

A head-first surface dive is usually performed while swimming breast stroke. From an extended position the arms are swept backwards, the head and shoulders are thrust downwards and the body is bent sharply at the hips. This causes the body to rotate, the movement being assisted by scooping the arms forwards and downwards. As a result, the legs are raised and the body, becoming vertical, sinks under its own weight. A return to the surface is effected by crouching on the floor of the pool and springing upwards.

Surface diving, feet-first *(see fig. 47)*

A feet-first surface dive is made from a vertical position while treading water. By making a powerful downward thrust with the legs and arms, the body is forced upwards and out of the water. With the arms held at the sides or extended upwards, the body will sink under its own weight. A return to the surface can be made as for the **Head-first surface dive** (see above).

Fig. 47: Surface diving, feet-first

Robinson Crusoe

One side of the pool is designated 'island', and the other side 'shipwreck'. Swimmers have to retrieve items from the 'shipwreck' to be taken to the 'island'. Variations can be introduced by:

- climbing out to select the item to be carried
- carrying the item above the water surface
- varying the number of items to be carried, e.g. one at a time or collectively
- varying the number of trips to complete the transfer.

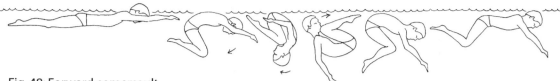

Fig. 48: Forward somersault

Fig. 49: Backward somersault

Forward somersault *(see fig. 48)*

From a prone floating position, the back is rounded, the knees are brought towards the chest and the head is dropped to bring the body into a tightly tucked position. As the body begins to rotate, the arms scoop downwards and backwards, maintaining pressure towards the feet until the rotation has been completed and the body begins to return to the starting position.

Backward somersault *(see fig. 49)*

From a supine floating position, the back is rounded, the knees are drawn towards the chest and the head is tucked to bring the chin towards the chest. This causes the body to assume a compact ball shape. The body now rotates backwards as the arms scull forwards, towards the feet. Sculling pressure is maintained until the body is upright again and moving into the starting position.

Fig. 50: Sailing boat

Sailing boat *(see fig. 50)*

While sculling head-first, one leg is bent at the knee so that the foot is drawn up in line with the opposite knee and is held in position while travel is continued. The upraised knee resembles the shape of a sail and pupils can be encouraged to change sails while on the move.

Water snail *(see fig. 51)*

While sculling head-first, the knees are drawn up to the chest to a tuck position. Then the legs are extended again and the sequence is repeated by alternating the body positions.

Fig. 51: Water snail

Motley race

By selecting different ways of travelling, such as those described in previous pages, an interesting and challenging sequence can be devised for swimmers to perform while travelling from one part of the pool to another. The following are examples of the skills which might be included:

- push off and glide into sculling head-first – 10 metres
- tuck and spin, followed by sculling feet-first – 5 metres
- rotate to a prone position and perform the canoe – 5 metres
- spin around to swim feet-first to the finish.

Distances can be indicated by placing suitable markers on the poolside.

Sequences

Having acquired some of the water skills previously described, pupils can now be encouraged to make up their own sequences of two or more activities, attempting to make smooth transitions from one to the other, e.g.:

- sculling feet-first → tuck to washing tub 1½ turns → sculling feet-first
- sculling head-first → rotate sideways into canoe → surface dive
- push and glide from the poolside → forward somersault → level out and scull feet-first.

ACTIVITIES AND GAMES WITH A PARTNER

In addition to the activities listed below, some of those described in Chapter 3 may be adapted for use by pupils who are swimmers. An example of this adaptation is **Two dogs and a bone** below (see also **Cycling** on page 11).

Two dogs and a bone

The two players in this game, about two metres apart, are treading water with a small floating object – e.g. a ball or a quoit – placed between them. Each attempts to snatch away the object and swim to the nearest side of the pool without being tagged by the other.

Rolling the log (see fig. 52)

Partner no. 1 assumes a back floating position, with no. 2 standing alongside. No. 1 then attempts to roll around sideways by tensing the body on one side, turning the head and pulling over the opposite shoulder in the same direction. As the movement begins, no. 2 assists with support under the shoulders and hips. Later this can be performed without support by sculling with the hands by the sides to assist rotation and balance.

Thigh balance (see fig. 53)

The partners face each other, clasping each other's hands firmly. No. 1, acting as support, stands with feet apart and knees bent, and leans backwards with body braced. No. 2 steps forwards carefully to take up a balanced position, with his feet on the thighs of the supporter. After the balanced position has been held for a short time, the grip is released, allowing no. 2 to perform a backward glide. Pairs must be well spaced to avoid collisions.

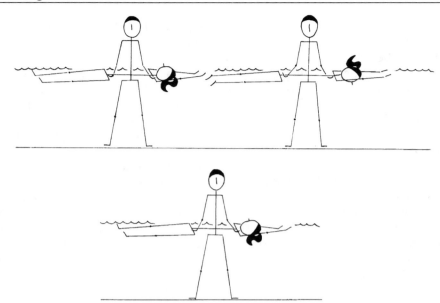

Fig. 52: Rolling the log

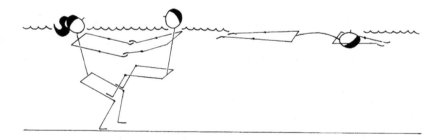

Fig. 53: Thigh balance

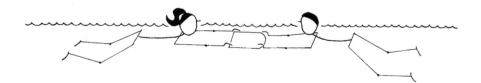

Fig. 54: Hoop push

Hoop tug of war

Partners take up a position on the opposite sides of a strong plastic hoop. Holding it with one hand and using an appropriate stroke, each tries to pull his partner along.

Hoop push *(see fig. 54)*

Each partner is in a prone position, grasping the opposite side of a hoop with both hands. One attempts to push the other backwards by kicking strongly. A short pole or a barbell float may be used instead of a hoop. The type of leg kick may be nominated or a free choice may be given.

Swimming with hoop

Interesting partner sequences and movement patterns can be evolved by the swimmers using a hoop as a focal point and swimming to, from or around it. To add to the possibilities, the hoop may also be held with the hands or the feet.

Diving and swimming through hoops

Interesting sequences can be devised by each of the swimmers, in turn, holding a hoop or hoops for the other to dive or swim through. Hoops may be held either vertically or flat, on or below the water surface.

Tandem swimming, back stroke *(see fig. 55)*

Swimmers are in a back floating position, one behind the other, the front swimmer being towed by the rear swimmer.

Alternatively, the rear partner hooks his feet lightly under the armpits of the one in front. When comfortably and securely in position, both then travel head-first using sculling actions (*see fig. 56*), modified back crawl (*see fig. 57*) or elementary back stroke arm actions. It should be noted that the leader can use only arms, with the rear swimmer providing extra propulsion by using a leg action. Elementary back stroke is performed with a kick similar to an inverted breast stroke, the arms being used to make very wide sculling actions.

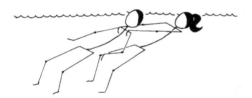

Fig. 55: Tandem swimming, back stroke

Fig. 56: Tandem swimming using sculling actions

Fig. 57: Tandem swimming using modified back crawl

Fig. 58: Tandem, swimming front crawl

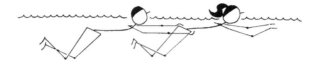

Fig. 59: Tandem swimming, breast stroke

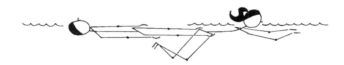

Fig. 60: Tug boat

Tandem swimming, front crawl *(see fig. 58)*

In this form of tandem swimming, the swimmers are in a prone position. The one in front hooks his feet lightly under the arms and across the back of the one at the rear. Both now use a modified front crawl arm action, but only the rear swimmer can use the leg action.

Tandem swimming, breast stroke *(see fig. 59)*

The swimmers are positioned as for **Tandem swimming, front crawl** (see above), but with the rear swimmer holding the hips of the one in front. The front swimmer uses both arms and legs, but the rear swimmer can use only the legs. To simplify breathing and to avoid the leader kicking his partner, a slightly more upright body position than usual is needed.

Tug boat *(see fig. 60)*

The swimmers take up position, one behind the other in this activity. The one in front is in a prone position while the one at the rear assumes a back-floating position, using his feet to grasp the waist of his partner. When comfortably attached, towing begins, with the swimmer at the front using breast stroke.

Shunting

The partners start by facing each other and treading water. No. 1 places his hands on the shoulders of no. 2, who begins to swim breast stroke. As he does so, no. 1 moves into a supine position to be pushed or shunted along head-first. After covering a short distance, both swimmers resume treading water and the roles are reversed, with no. 1 swimming breast stroke and no. 2 being pushed. In order to facilitate the action, the one who is being pushed must keep his arms straight and must lie back in the water.

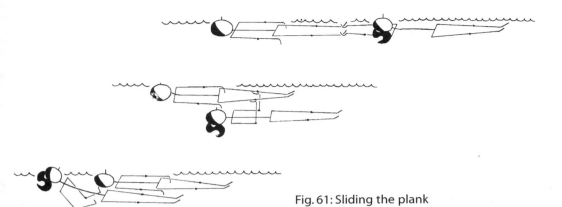

Fig. 61: Sliding the plank

Sliding the plank (see fig. 61)

Both swimmers take up a back floating position, one behind the other to begin with. The one in front reaches overhead to grasp the ankles of his partner and, moving under water, pulls and pushes him along the surface to change positions. The one who is being pulled assists by sculling feet-first. The actions continue, with one pulling and one sculling alternately, and several changes of position are attempted.

Chinese boxing (see fig. 62)

Partners face each other and tread water. Using the left hand, each grasps his partner's right wrist, allowing the hand to be free. From this position each tries to tap his partner lightly on the head using the right hand. The game can be quite tiring and should be of fairly short duration.

Mirror swimming

Partners swim side by side and attempt to match swimming strokes or various water skills in form and time. The forms to be attempted may be designated by the teacher or swimmers may be given a free choice, e.g.:

- swimming front crawl side by side, modifying the breathing pattern so that partners can see each other during inhalation
- swimming breast stroke – rotating to a supine position from the glide and continuing by sculling head-first.

Meeting and parting

Movement patterns can be created in which partners meet and part in similar or dissimilar style – sometimes, perhaps, to conjoin in a specific skill, e.g.:

- push from opposite sides of the pool, swim underwater to meet halfway across, then surface together
- approach from a distance, meet with a surface dive and rise together.

Fig. 62: Chinese boxing

Fig. 63: Towing

Towing *(see fig. 63)*

In this activity pupils operate in pairs, trying to discover ways of towing each other through the water using:
- various one-handed grips
- a short stick, rope or hoop, etc.

Different strokes may be used and the activity can be competitive over stated distances.

Passing in twos

Partners are in free formation, each pair with a ball, and treading water. Each couple then attempts to make the greatest number of consecutive passes without dropping the ball. The type of pass may be specified or players may be given a free choice from:
- two-handed passing
- one-handed passing or volleying.

Punching or holding the ball should not be permitted.

Over and under

Partners face each other in shoulder deep water, no. 1 with feet astride and arms stretched sideways. No. 2 performs a surface dive over one arm and then swims between his partner's legs, before resurfacing to repeat the sequence over the other arm. Having returned to the starting position to complete the sequence, the positions are changed. This may be used as a competitive activity with the whole class arranged in pairs and well spread out.

Scissors *(see fig. 64)*

Partners start in a front or back floating position, in line and head to head, with arms extended to grasp each other's hands. From this position they move their legs and arms sideways, thus opening to a star position and drawing their heads together. A gentle leg flutter may be used in the early stages to assist a horizontal position in the water.

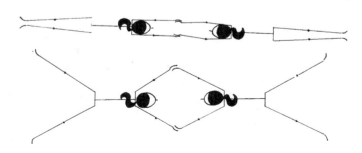

Fig. 64: Scissors

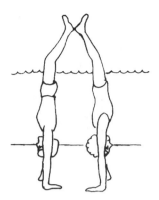

Fig. 65: Partner handstand

Partner handstand *(see fig. 65)*

Once they have mastered a handstand on their own, pupils can be introduced to handstands in twos. One pupil performs a handstand and his partner, facing him, then does likewise. The aim is for the two to place the bottoms of their feet together above the water and hold the position briefly.

GAMES FOR SMALL GROUPS

Waiters' race

Starting in the water and holding a floatboard on the palm of one hand to represent a waiter's tray, swimmers attempt to be first across the pool without dropping the 'tray'.

Trellis *(see fig. 66)*

In groups of three and upwards, the swimmers are arranged in line, side by side and with heads and feet alternating. Each takes up a back floating position, using a stationary sculling action. When all are ready, the swimmers reach out to grasp the ankles of those on either side of them. From this position the swimmers then extend their arms and feet gently sideways in unison to produce a trellis shape. Actions should be carried out slowly and deliberately to maintain balance.

Chinese wall (2) *(see fig. 67)*

All the players are at one side of the pool except for one chosen to be the defender, who treads water in the middle, in a marked out area two metres wide. The others then attempt to swim across the pool without being tagged by the person in the middle.

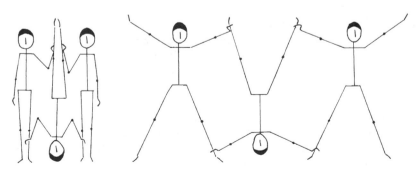

Fig. 66: Trellis

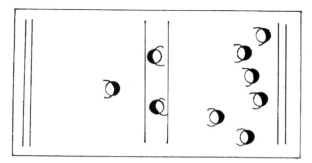

Fig. 67: Chinese wall (2)

Those who are tagged join the centre player to act as defenders. The last 'untagged' player is the winner.

Underwater tag

In this game of tag, the person chosen to be 'It' can only tag the rest of the group by submerging to do so. Those tagged must stand still in shallow water, in an astride position. If any of those still free swims under their legs this frees them again. Every few minutes a new person should be chosen to become 'It'.

Follow the leader (2)

One member of the group, designated as the leader, starts off and performs a variety of skills and stunts, e.g. rotation swimming, somersaults, head-first sculling etc. Everyone else in the group follows and attempts to copy what the leader does. Pupils should take turns to act as leader.

Whitewater swimming (see fig. 68)

This is an activity best used with a large group of swimmers, arranged in two facing lines a few metres apart. Each holds a floatboard, edgeways on to the water. On a given signal they start to push these backwards and forwards vigorously to create rough water in the space between the lines. Pupils then take it in turns to try to swim through the 'whitewater rapids' from one end of the line to the other, without stopping or standing up.

Fig. 68: Whitewater swimming

Pigeon race

Pupils line up on one side of the pool. On the signal to go they jump or dive in and swim to the opposite side, climbing out to sit on the side. The one who is first to 'reach the pigeon loft' wins. Variety may be introduced by stipulating the stroke to be swum, or making the race more difficult by stating that only one arm (to represent a broken wing) may be used.

Fig. 69: Threading the needle

Threading the needle (see fig. 69)

This is an activity for three pupils, two of whom face each other, holding hands to form a small circle. The third swimmer then attempts to dive through the circle using a porpoise-type dive. After each attempt the swimmers change places, so that each has a try.

Ball passing

This is a game which can be played either in twos or in small groups. While players are treading water and are some distance apart from each other, a ball is passed from one to another by catching and throwing, using two hands or one hand only. Each group counts the number of consecutive passes made before the ball is dropped. Subsequent attempts can then be made to beat that number or to surpass the score of the other groups.

Ball passing contest

This game is a development of **Ball passing** (see above). The ball is passed among the players, who try to make as many consecutive passes as possible before the teacher stops the game. If the ball is dropped, counting must restart from the beginning. The game can be varied by designating the type of passing to be used. The team making the greatest number of passes wins.

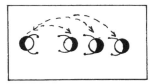

Fig. 70: Ten trips

Ten trips

The players are arranged in lines of three, all treading water. A ball is passed in sequence from no. 1 to no. 2 and then to no. 3. The ball is returned to no. 1 over the head of no. 2 by no. 3 and this represents one 'trip'. The first team to do this ten times is the winner.

A variation is played in fours (see fig. 70). Three players are arranged in a line, one behind the other, with a fourth player facing them and holding a ball. The ball is thrown to every player in turn, starting with no. 1, and is returned to the thrower each time. After the last player's return has been made, the thrower calls out 'One' to indicate that one trip has been made. The first to complete a given number of trips is the winner.

Team passing

The teacher arranges the class into teams of equal number and decides which team should begin. The players in that team then try to make as many passes as possible, while members of the opposing team attempt to intercept. If the ball is dropped on the water or is intercepted by the other side, then that side gains possession. Each team's passes should be counted and after a given period of time the one which has made the most consecutive passes wins.

Skittle guard

The players are arranged in circles, each group surrounding a floating hoop placed in the centre. One player is the guard and must try to prevent the others from throwing a ball so that it lands inside the hoop or hits a skittle inside it. A player who succeeds in scoring in this way changes places with the guard. Players should be encouraged to pass the ball quickly from one to the other before attempting to score.

Hoop ball *(see fig. 71)*

Having played **Hoop guard** (see page 22) and **Team passing** (see page 43), players can now graduate to this game in which two teams compete. Hoops are placed at each end of the playing area and the object is to pass and throw a ball to get it in the opponents' hoop. Each team has a hoop guard who also restarts

the game after a goal has been conceded by throwing the ball to a member of his own team.

Circle gap passing *(see fig. 72)*

Five players are arranged in a circle at double-arm distance apart. One player is in the centre of the circle with a ball. The ball is thrown to a player in the circle who returns it to the one in the middle before swimming outside the circle to the next space on the right to receive and return the ball again. This procedure is continued until the swimmer has returned to his original place. Then the other players, in turn, do the same. In competitive form, the first team to complete the circuit wins.

Corner spry (2) *(see fig. 73)*

This is a variation of **Corner spry (1)** (see page 23). Each team is arranged in a line,

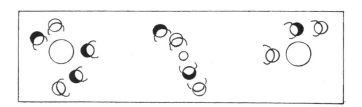

Fig. 71: Hoop ball

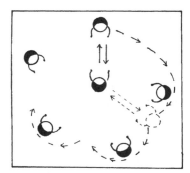

Fig. 72: Circle gap passing

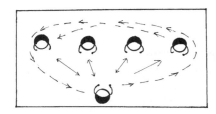

Fig. 73: Corner spry (2)

facing one player (the thrower) standing some three metres away and holding a ball. The ball is thrown and is then returned by each player in turn down the line. When the last player receives the ball, he and the thrower have to swim round the back of the team so that the previous thrower becomes the first in line and the last player becomes the thrower. Meanwhile, the players in line move one place sideways and play continues in the same way until all players have returned to their original positions. For added interest, the style of passing can be designated, and if played with one-handed passes the game can be good practice for water polo.

Newcombe (2)
This game is a simplified form of volleyball in which the ball may also be caught, but not always volleyed. The teams are separated by a net (or suspended rope). The object is to propel the ball over the net so that it hits the water in the opposing side's court. The game is started by a throw from the base line which may pass directly over the net or it may be played by three other players, the last of whom must pass it over. Each team serves in turn, after each break in play. Up to three passes are allowed before either team returns the ball over the net. Points are scored and the service changes when:
- the service fails
- the receiving side allows the ball to hit the water, or if the players do not return the ball over the net after three passes have been made
- if the ball passes under the net or goes out of bounds.

Archball cricket
This is a modified form of cricket in which there are two small teams, one batting and one fielding. One team is in line for hitting,

the other spreads out for fielding. A player from the fielding side acts as a bowler and, using a soft ball, bowls it to the first in line of the batting side. As the ball is hit with an open hand, all of the fielding side move into a line, one behind the other, at the place where the ball alights or is caught. They then begin to pass the ball overhead from one to another. At the same time, the hitter swims from base to a designated nearby point as many times as possible before the fielding side has passed the ball to the end of the line. The number of swims (runs) is counted and the players reposition themselves to continue the game. When each member of the hitting side has had a turn, the teams change over. The winner is the team with the greatest number of swims (runs). The ball must be hit inside the area of the pool. If batted on to the poolside, no score can be counted.

Horses and jockeys (2)
The players are arranged in a circle in pairs, one behind the other, with those in the rear mounted on the backs of those in front. On a signal, the 'jockeys' dismount, swim around the circle in a clockwise direction and finally pass through their partners' legs before remounting. The winner is the first player back in position. Players change places after each contest, so that the 'horses' then become the 'jockeys'. The circle should be large enough to avoid any collisions when remounting.

Jousting
The players are in free formation in pairs; one from each pair is mounted on the back of his partner of similar size. When all are comfortably and securely mounted, a signal is given and one 'knight' attempts to unseat another by pulling and pushing. This is an enjoyable activity, but it requires careful

supervision. Shoulder-deep water should be used and over-boisterous actions should be prohibited. To avoid collision, players should be well spaced out. Only one 'knight' should engage another and frequent changes of mount should be made.

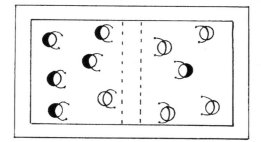

Fig. 75: Scout

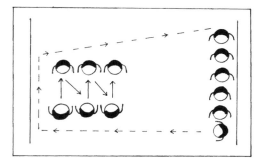

Fig. 74: Team swimming v. ball passing

Team swimming v. ball passing (see fig. 74)

Team A is arranged in a file, with players placed one behind the other. Team B is positioned nearby in two lines, with players facing each other, some four metres apart. At the starting signal, Team A swim, one at a time, around Team B. At the same time the players in Team B pass a ball continuously across and down the lines in a zig-zag fashion. When all the players of Team A have completed the circuit and are back in their original places, the passing stops and the number of passes is noted. Places are then changed and the team which has made the most passes wins. Adjustments of numbers and of the swimming circuit can be made to suit the conditions and abilities of the swimmers.

Scout (see fig. 75)

The teams are arranged in opposite halves of the playing area with a neutral space between them. This may be indicated by markers on the poolside or by a line of floating hoops. No players from either team are allowed to go inside the neutral area. Each team has a 'scout' in the opposing team's territory who is free to move around. The object of the game is for a team to make clean passes to the 'scout', using a large ball, while the opposing team try to prevent this by intercepting. The number of 'scouts' may be varied, if desired. The winning team is the one making the greatest number of passes in a given time.

Fig. 76: Pig in the middle

Pig in the middle (see fig. 76)

Two players, one with a playball, face each other. They should be about two or three metres apart, with a third player standing midway between them. The outside players then pass the ball between them, while the middle player tries to intercept. If successful, he changes place with the thrower.

Traffic lights

The players start in free formation and treading water. When the colours of the traffic lights are called out, the players respond as follows:

- *red* – stationary sculling
- *amber* – treading water
- *green* – swimming freely around.

The intention is to keep the players alert whilst allowing them to practise well-known skills.

Crows and cranes

This is a variation of **Crusts and crumbs** on page 14. Players take up position in the middle of the pool, standing back to back in two parallel lines about one metre apart. One of the lines is named 'Crows' and the other, 'Cranes'. When either name is called out, those in that line immediately swim to their side of the pool, while the others turn round and swim after them in an attempt to tag them before they can reach it. The caller can keep the players alert by prolonging the first syllable, i.e. 'Crrr . . . ', before completing the name, or by using another name with the same first syllable, e.g. 'Crrrr . . . ackers!'

Sting ray

A number of 'safe' bases are arranged around the pool. One player chosen to be 'Sting ray' performs a stationary scull in the middle of the pool, while the other players swim around cautiously, attempting to touch him. If they succeed, a point is awarded. Suddenly, 'Sting ray' gives chase and tries to tag the others before they have reached the safety of a base. Any players who are tagged become 'Sting rays' in the middle. There are two winners in this game: the last one to be tagged and the one who makes the most touches. The bases may be indicated by placing markers on the poolside or by using floating hoops.

Live fishing

The players are arranged in circles and are numbered, e.g. 1 to 6. One player who has a slow sinking object, such as a diving disc or plastic quoit, drops it in the middle, at the same time calling out a number. The player with that number has then to surface dive and try to catch the object before it reaches the bottom of the pool. He, in turn, drops the object in the middle of the circle and calls out another number, and the game proceeds. The aim should be to make sure that all players have an equal number of chances to recover the object. Points may be awarded for successful catches.

Scatter dodge ball (2)

The players form a large circle, each treading water and numbered consecutively. The teacher tosses a soft ball into the circle and calls out a number. The player with that number has to retrieve the ball while the others scatter by swimming off in various directions. When the player has collected the ball he calls out 'Stop!' and the others remain where they are, treading water. The player in possession then tries to hit one of the others with the ball and if successful the hit player forfeits a 'life'. The winner is the player who loses the fewest of a given number of 'lives' during the game. The game is restarted after each attempt to hit a player, whether this is successful or not.

Over and under the legs

The swimmers, preferably in small teams of four or five, first take up position in line, side by side and about two metres apart. They assume a back floating position, using a stationary scull. On the signal to start, no. 1 turns to perform a surface dive over the legs of no. 2, then swims under no. 3, surface dives over the legs of the next in line, and so on, after which return is made to the starting position by swimming. No. 2 follows suit, travelling in the same direction, but returning to position by swimming under no. 1. The others in the team continue the sequence of over and under alternately, until the last player has returned to position. The first team to complete the circuit wins.

Obstacle races

In some races, as an alternative to swimming in certain styles or performing special skills, a course might be set out consisting of a series of obstacles to be negotiated, such as:

- surface diving over and swimming under ropes tied across the pool at water level
- touching balloons suspended from a rope placed across the pool at stretchable height
- swimming around buoyant objects, such as floats or hoops
- swimming through hoops suspended below the water surface
- picking up objects from the pool floor to be carried for a short distance
- collecting a ball to be dribbled, etc.

The number of obstacles will depend upon the availability of equipment, the distance to be covered and the degree of difficulty of each task. The course should be uncomplicated, easy to arrange and well within the physical capabilities of the swimmers. Obstacle courses can also be set out for use in relay races.

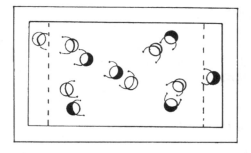

Fig. 77: End ball

Netball/basketball/skittleball/end ball

Using a variety of targets, team passing games can be devised, the object of which is to score by:

- throwing a ball into a net suspended in a circular buoy
- hitting a floating skittle placed inside a floating hoop
- passing a ball to a catcher or catchers located in a two-metre wide space at the end of the playing area (*see fig. 77*)
- aiming at targets placed on the poolside and guarded by a goalkeeper in the water.

Formation swimming (see fig. 78)

Having enjoyed the experience of swimming in co-ordination with a partner, further movement relationships are possible by working in small groups of at least four, using the same basic movements:

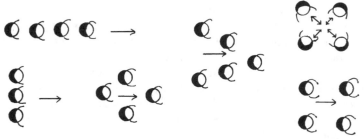

Fig. 78: Formation swimming

- meeting and parting
- travelling together
- interspersing the two above movements with various skills.

Given the opportunity, versatile and skilful swimmers will enjoy this type of water play. Those with particular aptitude can, eventually, graduate to the special disciplines of synchronised swimming.

RELAY RACES

Most people enjoy the zest and excitement which this type of competition produces. In most races swimmers compete to accumulate more points, to cover a course more quickly, or to complete tasks in a shorter time than their opponents. In some games all members of the team are active throughout, but in relay races only one member of the team is swimming at any one time.

Several of the competitive-type activities which have already been described in previous sections can be arranged in relay form, as illustrated in the examples which follow.

To maintain interest, to ease congestion at the starting and finishing points and to avoid waiting for turns, the teams should be small (two, three or four members) and the tasks which are set should be well within the capabilities of those competing. If and when entries are made from the poolside, the depth of water should be suitable and 'take-overs' should be carefully supervised (see pages 58 and 61).

Relay race rules

In all competitive events it is important that the rules, simple though they might be, should be clearly stated, fully understood and properly observed. This applies particularly in relay races in which starting, taking over and finishing are significant features. At the start swimmers should be allocated positions; they should remain still, and in a state of readiness, awaiting the signal to begin. For consistency, it is suggested that the official mode of starting be adopted: 'Take your marks . . . Go!' During take-overs, the incoming swimmer must touch the end of the course before the next one takes off, and at the termination the last swimmer must touch the end of the course in the designated manner. Not all take-overs are direct. Sometimes there are tasks to be performed in between, but nevertheless these should be performed correctly.

Restriction relay

Teams of up to four members are positioned at each side of the pool. In turn, each competitor swims across with a limb or limbs immobilised, e.g. no. l uses only one arm, no. 2 holds both legs together, no. 3 uses only his legs, etc.

Six ways across

A variation of **Restriction relay** (see above) is for each member of the team to swim across using any acceptable hybrid swimming stroke, e.g. breast stroke arm action with the front crawl leg action; back crawl stroke using a double arm action; rotation swimming (see page 31); swimming backwards or sideways, etc. The method of travel may be stated or teams may be allowed a free choice.

Rope towing relay

The teams line up on the poolside, with no. l in each team holding the end of a rope and the other end being held by the rest of the team. On the signal to start, no. l jumps into the water, still holding the rope, and swims across the pool. On touching the other side he is towed back to climb out. Then no. 2 takes over, and so on until the whole team is back on the poolside.

Fig. 79: Float relay

Float relay *(see fig. 79)*

At the start, the two halves of each team sit on opposite sides of the pool. No. 1 enters the water and holds a float at arms' length, ready to push off from the side on the signal to begin. The teams compete using legs only. As one swimmer starts, the next, on the opposite side, drops into the water ready to take over. Having completed a width, each swimmer hands over the float to the next to go and climbs out to sit on the poolside. The winning team is the one to have all its members sitting on the poolside after they have each completed their task. The same leg action may be used throughout or, to add variety, a different one may be used for each width.

Tunnel relay

Each team forms a line. Players stand one or two metres behind each other, with their feet wide apart. The rear member submerges to swim through the legs of all the others. When he has arrived and is standing at the front, with feet astride, the next swimmer follows suit, and so on until all the swimmers are back in their original places. The first team back in position wins.

Dribbling relay

Small teams (4–6 players) sit or stand on the poolside and a ball is placed in the water. At the start of the race no. 1 jumps into the water

to swim and dribble the ball to the opposite side. The ball is then thrown to land in the water in front of no. 2, who jumps in to follow suit. This process is repeated until the whole team has crossed over. After throwing the ball across, each team member climbs out to sit or stand on the poolside. The first team to complete the relay and finish on the poolside wins.

Exchange relay *(see fig. 80)*

The teams are divided so that half the members from each are at one side of the pool and the other half are at the opposite side. Players are positioned behind one another. The two front swimmers each take a different object (arm band, float, ball, etc.) to be exchanged in mid-pool before returning to hand it to the next in line, after which they move to the rear of the team. The procedure is followed until all players are back in their original places.

Clothes relay

The teams are of even numbers, with half of each team at opposite sides or ends of the pool, depending on the distance to be covered. No. 1 in each team wears pyjama trousers and, on the signal to start, dives or jumps in, swims to the end of the course, climbs out, undresses and hands the pyjamas to no. 2. No. 2 puts on the pyjamas and

Fig. 80: Exchange relay

swims to the opposite end where the procedure is repeated until the whole team is on the poolside with the clothing held aloft by no. 1.

Quoit relay

Teams of equal numbers are selected. Half the members from each are at one side of the pool and the other half, facing them, are at the opposite side. No. 1 in each team starts in the water, with a quoit balanced on his head. On the signal to start this team member attempts to swim the full width of the pool without the quoit falling off. At the other side the quoit is handed over to no. 2, who jumps in the water, balances it on his head and swims back across the pool. The race continues until all members of the team have completed the swim. A free choice of stroke is allowed, but if any swimmer drops the quoit, a point is lost. The first team standing on the poolside, having completed the course with no loss of points, or the fewest penalty points, wins.

5 • The Use of Music

In their natural play situations children often move to a rhythmic accompaniment, such as clapping, or sometimes with a vocal accompaniment, giving rise to singing games. They also enjoy playing with sound and music and adding their own movements, such as foot tapping. It seems reasonable to suggest, therefore, that such a movement–sound relationship can be used to add a further dimension to their experience in water.

In the early stages of getting used to the water, singing games and jingles can provide amusement as well as offering distraction from any feelings of apprehension which may be present. They are also good fun. The following are examples of well-known jingles or rhymes which may be used to encourage the pupils to build up their confidence and to practise useful skills through carrying out appropriate actions to the music.

1   *Ring-a Ring o' Roses . . .*
    Atishoo, atishoo   All blow bubbles
    We all fall down   Submerge

2   *This is the way we*
    Wash our face, ears . . .   With appropriate actions
    On a cold and frosty morning   Bobbing and shaking

3   *Bouncing balls go up and down*   Bobbing and springing
    Bouncing balls go round and round   Bounce, jumping and turning
    Bouncing balls go here and there   Bounce and jump sideways

4   *The wheels on the bus go round and round*   Sinking and stirring the water
    The people on the bus go up and down   Bobbing
    The windscreen wipers go swish, swish, swish   Arm sweeps in the water

5   *Head, shoulders, knees and toes*   Touch each part with two hands
    Draw a pattern with my nose   Draw shapes in the water

6   *Oranges and lemons*   Submerge to go under the arch

MUSICAL GAMES

Sound and music can also be used as a stimulus or accompaniment to a variety of games, such as the following.

Hokey cokey

The pupils form a circle, all singing and carrying out the appropriate actions in time.

Drum step

All the pupils start at one side and facing across the pool. To the accompaniment of a drum beat they attempt to cross. When the drum stops they must become still immediately and must remain so. Anyone moving must take a step backwards. The game continues until the first pupil crosses and touches the poolside.

Musical statues

Pupils move about freely in the water to the accompaniment of a drum or music. When the music stops they must adopt a statuesque pose. This may be nominated or a free choice may be allowed, e.g. shoulders under, arms forwards; arms sideways, one knee raised, etc. Alternatively, pupils may be asked to represent sportsmen or sportswomen or different kinds of occupations.

Musical hoops

Several floating hoops are spread around the shallow end of the pool. Whenever the music plays, the pupils move around. If it stops, they have to move to the nearest hoop and touch it. Subsequently, a hoop is removed, the music restarts and the game continues until only one hoop remains. This is a non-elimination game in which the fun is for all pupils to try to touch the last hoop.

SWIMMING WITH SOUND

When pupils can perform swimming strokes reasonably well, many of them will enjoy fitting their movements to the sound of a drum or to music. They will already be accustomed to the metrical rhythm of a six-beat leg kick in front and back crawl strokes and this can easily be accompanied by the sound of a drum played by the teacher or leader. Once a sound–movement relationship has been established, it can be fun matching swimming movements to clearly defined musical beats in 4/4 (march time) or 3/4 (waltz time) from a drum, or through using topical music such as the 'Match of the Day' theme or 'Messin' about on the River'. As experience grows, other rhythms can be introduced with a wider variety of swimming movements. Teachers and pupils will inter-pret music in different ways but three examples are given for guidance.

- **Head-first scull**   1, 2, 3, 4 – 1, 2, 3, 4 etc.
- **Stationary scull**   1, 2, 3, 4 – 1, 2, 3, 4 etc.
- **Feet-first scull**   1, 2, 3, 4 – 1, 2, 3, 4 etc.

Accentuate the first or alternate beats of each bar to indicate the changes of direction of the hand movements.

- **Breaststroke** 1, 2, 3   1, 2, 3   1, 2, 3   1, 2, 3
    pull   _glide_   _pull_   _glide_

- **Rotation from front to back crawl** – 1½ cycles of each stroke in 3/4 time:

    pull 2, 3   _pull_ 2, 3   _pull_ 2, 3
    roll and pull 2, 3   _pull_ 2, 3   _pull_ 2, 3

SAFETY

If music is used, battery-operated equipment is recommended. Electrical equipment on a poolside can be dangerous. It should be safe, appropriately situated and have the approval of the pool management. Interest in this type of recreational activity and its development can lead to synchronised swimming, a branch of the sport which is becoming increasingly popular. For further reading on this subject, please refer to the Bibliography.

6 • Entries

In the chapter dealing with individual activities for non-swimmers, mention has already been made of various ways in which pupils might get into the water for the purpose of starting to swim. Later, however, as progress is made, entries themselves can become a pleasurable preoccupation, leading eventually to the development of diving skills.

Among the various actions which most children enjoy performing is jumping. Their natural exuberance often expresses itself in jumping for the sheer joy of it and many of their games activities, e.g. skipping, hopscotch and giant strides, involve jumping of one sort or another. In free or unsupervised play in a swimming pool they can be observed launching themselves into the water in a variety of ways and obviously enjoying the exhilaration of flight. Even those who cannot swim will find ways of jumping in, providing they can make a safe landing and regain balance afterwards.

In the controlled situation of the swimming lesson, advantage can be taken of this love of jumping to introduce and develop a series of entry skills complementary to the work in the water. In so doing there are three stages to consider:
- movement experience in the water
- feet-first entries from the poolside
- head-first entries from the poolside, leading up to the plunge dive, the most usual form of entry adopted by recreational swimmers.

MOVEMENT EXPERIENCE IN THE WATER

Depending upon the stage reached and the type of entries to be attempted, it is important for pupils to have gained confidence through practising certain basic skills, mostly in water of standing depth. These should include practices requiring them to:
- keep their eyes open under water
- control breathing and glide (see fig. 81)
- spring upwards from the pool floor (see fig. 82)
- turn upside down in the water, resurface and tread water (see figs 83 and 84).

Many of the activities detailed in previous chapters, e.g. **Pushing and gliding** (see page 12), **Handstands** (see page 28) and **Somersaults** (see page 34), should have helped them to acquire the experience necessary to progress to poolside entries.

FEET-FIRST ENTRIES

Knowing that they are capable of a safe landing and that they can control their balance in the water, children will enjoy jumping in from the poolside.

The aim and purpose of feet-first entries is to develop the ability to spring into the air, to control the body in the air and to experience the sensation of flight. The practices on pages 57–8 will be found useful in achieving these aims.

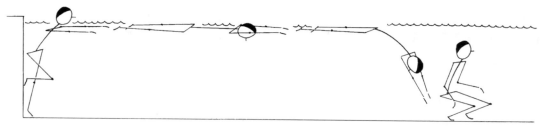

Fig. 81: Control breathing and glide underwater

Fig. 82: Spring upwards from the pool floor

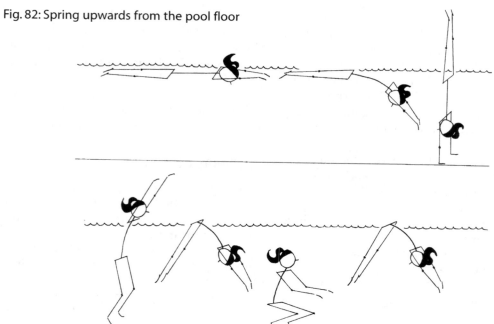

Figs 83 and 84: Turn upside down in the water, resurface and tread water

1 Stand on the poolside, with toes gripping the edge and arms at the side of the body. Keep the body upright and step forwards to enter the water with legs together.

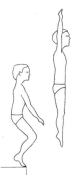

Fig. 85

2 As for (1), but with a preparatory bending of the knees and an upward spring from both feet (*see fig. 85*).

3 Stand as before, but during an upward and forward jump make shapes in the air – e.g. thin, wide, tucked or twisted – and make the entry with both feet together.

Fig. 86: Bomb entry

4 Stand on the poolside and jump forwards to assume a tucked position by drawing the knees towards the chest and clasping them with the forearms. In this position the water is met with both feet and seat and a 'bomb'-type entry is made (*see fig. 86*). This is one of the techniques used for **Safe entry** into the water (see page 68).

Fig. 87: Straddle jump

5 Stand, and then jump forwards with a single foot take-off, keeping one leg forward and one leg backward and the arms held forwards and sideways. In this jump, called the **Straddle jump**, effort should be made to keep the head above the water on entry by using a scissor kick as the legs reach the water (*see fig. 87*). This is also one of the techniques used for **Safe entry** into the water (see page 68).

6 Stand, then jump forwards with a single foot take-off and run in the air before making a feet-first entry.

Fig. 88

7 Stand, then jump upwards and forwards, and turn in the air. The movement can be assisted by turning the head and moving one arm across the body in the same direction (*see fig. 88*).

Fig. 89

8 From a standing position, use an upward and forward jump and tuck in the air before stretching the body into a straight position for a feet-first entry (*see fig. 89*).

Fig. 90

9 From a standing position, make an upward and forward jump and then attempt to reach down and touch the shins with the finger tips before stretching the body upright prior to entry (*see fig. 90*).

10 From a standing position, pupils are now encouraged to create their own jumps.

HEAD-FIRST ENTRIES

In teaching diving from the poolside, special precautions are necessary. The Amateur Swimming Association and the Swimming Teachers Association advocate that for both adults and children, the water depth should be ideally their full standing height plus arms and fingers fully extended. However, this advice must be considered exemplary as very few existing swimming pools can provide water of sufficient depth to meet this requirement for adults or tall children. The majority of modern pools have a deep end of only 1.8 metres and no diving pit. It can only be suggested that this guidance be followed where possible and that where it is not practicable, the deepest water available should be used with the exercise of additional caution.

Diving in Swimming Pool, *Institute of Bath and Recreational Managers et al.*

Inevitably, as progress is made and confidence grows, pupils will wish to learn how to enter the water head-first. They will already be accustomed to being upside down and gliding with arms and head leading, having previously experienced such skills as gliding, surface diving and rotating. Through their feet-first entries they will also have experienced the take-off, flight and entry into the water. The following skills have been found effective in encouraging children to make simple head-first entries and will lead eventually to a plunge dive.

Fig. 91: Crouch roll

Fig. 93: Kneeling dive

Crouch roll *(see fig. 91)*

From a crouch position on the poolside, toes gripping the edge, the body is tucked into a rounded shape, the head is kept down and the lower legs are held with the hands. While still holding this tucked position, pupils roll into the water.

Fig. 92: Sitting dive

Sitting dive *(see fig. 92)*

Pupils sit on the edge of the pool, feet resting on the rail or scum trough, and knees and feet together. The upper arms are held against the ears and the chin is pushed towards the chest. By raising the hips and leaning forwards slightly, the body will start to overbalance. At this point a gentle push is made by the feet, the entry being such that the body passes through a 'hole' made by the hands.

Kneeling dive *(see fig. 93)*

A kneeling position is taken up by the side of the pool, one knee resting almost up to the edge and the toes of the other foot gripping the pool edge firmly. The toes of the rear foot should be curled under, providing a firm base for the push-off. The arms should be stretched beyond the head, with the upper arms against the ears. The body is now bent forwards so that the shoulder touches the bent knee. Entry is made by rolling forwards. Pupils should ensure that the head is kept down and the legs are extended. The aim should be to reach for the bottom of the pool.

Fig. 94: Crouch dive

Crouch dive *(see fig. 94)*

The start is from a crouch position, with the knees together, and the arms extended and held closely against the sides of the head. With the chin pushed towards the chest and the arms pointed downwards towards the point of entry, the body is allowed to overbalance with a push to reach for the bottom of the pool.

Fig. 95: High crouch dive

Fig. 97: Plunge dive

High crouch dive *(see fig. 95)*

A more upright stance than that for the **Crouch dive** (see previous page) is adopted, so that the knees are bent and the trunk leans forwards at an angle of approximately 45 degrees. The arms are extended and pressed against the ears, with the hands together. From this position, a vigorous push is made into an upward and outward flight, with the body entering the water fully stretched, toes pointed.

Fig. 96: Lunge dive

Lunge dive *(see fig. 96)*

One leg is forwards, slightly bent at the knee, and toes grip the edge of the pool. The other leg is also slightly bent and supported on the ball of the foot. The head and arm positions are the same as for the **High crouch dive** (see above). A push is made from the forward leg, causing the body to overbalance. During flight the legs are brought together and the body is fully stretched so that a clean entry is made.

Plunge dive *(see fig. 97)*

This dive starts from a position with the feet slightly apart, toes gripping the edge of the pool. The knees are bent and the upper body is horizontal, the back being slightly rounded. The arms hang loosely downwards so that the stance is comfortable, balanced and relaxed. The eyes look forwards at the intended point of entry. As the body is allowed to over-balance and move towards the water, the arms are swung forwards into line with the body, and at the same time the ankles, knees and hips are extended in a vigorous push. The arms reach for entry, with the body maintaining a stretched and streamlined position until it has passed completely beneath the surface of the water.

This dive may be adapted and used in competitions, the angle of entry depending upon the stroke being executed. In general, the entry for front crawl is fairly shallow so that a speedy return is made to the surface, allowing the swimmer to move quickly into the stroke. In breast stroke and butterfly events, however, a deeper entry is desirable so that use can be made of the underwater leg action permitted in these strokes.

SAFETY

In all the entries from the poolside it is important that pupils are aware of and obey the following rules at all times:

- ensure that the water is clear before leaving the poolside
- keep well spaced so that there is no risk of collision
- keep the toes over the edge of the pool so that they grip firmly
- treat the poolside with caution, since it is often slippery
- in all feet-first entries keep the head up and look ahead
- move forwards after resurfacing to avoid obstructing other persons' entries (this is important when setting off in 'cannon' or all together)
- ensure that the water depth is adequate for the activity being performed (see page 58)

- for head-first entries the arms should be extended beyond the head (the head is held in its normal position and the upper arms are held against the ears).

All the foregoing activities are important preliminaries for the more stylised forms of diving which may be attempted later. In the early stages, style and technique are of little interest, since children merely want to enjoy the action. Nevertheless, in doing so they are gaining in personal skill and good habits should be encouraged as soon as possible. For those who are interested in teaching the techniques and developing diving as a specialised activity with competition in mind, reference should be made to the appropriate section dealing with diving in the Bibliography.

7 • An Introduction to Water Polo

Although there are many team games which can be played in water, only one has been developed into an officially recognised major game and that is water polo.

It is a particularly strenuous game to play well and all players have to be strong and versatile in the water. They need to be able to change direction quickly to reverse, to rotate from front to back, to swim very quickly in short bursts and to tread water for long periods. In addition, they need to be able to project themselves high above the water surface to receive and pass the ball and to shoot for goal. Water polo has traditionally been regarded as a game for men and boys, but today women and girls are being encouraged to play.

Water polo is a team-passing game similar to football, netball or handball. Each side has seven players including a goalkeeper, but four substitutes are allowed, making a total of eleven. The duration of play is four quarters of five minutes each, with an interval of two minutes between each period, during which the teams change ends. Before the start, the teams line up at opposite ends of the pool. On the starting signal the players swim towards the ball which is thrown into the centre of the pool by the referee. Subsequently, movement of the players within the designated playing area is free. If a goal is scored, the teams reposition anywhere in their own halves of the playing area. Play is then resumed by one member of the team that has conceded the goal passing the ball from the centre line to another member of his team. However, at the beginning of each new quarter, teams line up as they do at the commencement of the game. Apart from the goalkeeper, players may use only one hand in contact with the ball. The ball must not be taken underwater and it must not be fisted. Body contact is not allowed unless the opponent is actually holding the ball.

In addition to these few basic rules, there are many other details and rules which are beyond the scope of this book, but further information may be obtained by reference to books dealing specifically with water polo, such as those listed in the Bibliography.

Water polo, like many other games, has become quite complex, with the introduction of additional rules and regulations to ensure fair play. However, it is possible to modify these so that players of varying abilities can participate quite successfully.

A SIMPLIFIED VERSION OF WATER POLO

Having played some of the games already described in previous chapters of this book, pupils should now have acquired sufficient water skills to be able to play simplified forms of water polo. As an introduction, simple rules such as those suggested below should suffice:

- the game may be played with more or fewer than the normal seven in each team
- before the start the teams line up across opposite ends of the pool
- the game is started by a referee blowing a whistle and throwing the ball into the centre of the pool
- each team swims towards the ball in an attempt to gain possession and to begin a series of passes before shooting at the opponents' goal
- any player in possession of the ball must either pass or shoot at goal when touched by an opponent
- apart from the goalkeepers, the players must swim or tread water when in possession of the ball. If a player is impeded or pushed underwater, a free throw is awarded to that player
- jumping from the bottom of the pool or standing when holding the ball is an offence, resulting in a free throw to the nearest player of the opposing team
- if the ball is thrown out of play, a free throw is awarded to the opposing team, to be taken at the point nearest to where the ball went out of play

- the ball must not be taken underwater. A free throw is given to the opposing team if this offence is committed
- when a goal is scored, both teams move into their own halves of the pool and the game is restarted by the centre player of the team against which the goal was scored passing the ball to one of his teammates
- the teams should change ends at half-time
- each half should be of relatively short duration, e.g. 5–10 minutes, because the game is a strenuous one.

As the players become more skilful and adept at this modified form of the game, progress can be made by introducing more of the official rules. Time can also be spent practising specific skills, the application of which will lead to greater enjoyment by those participating.

SOME USEFUL SKILLS

Treading water

A water polo player has to spend a good deal of time treading water during a game while catching, throwing or rising out of the water to throw. The most effective method is by using the **'egg-beater' kick** (*see fig. 98*). The body is held in an upright position, with

Fig. 98: Treading water – the 'egg-beater' kick

the legs bent. As the name implies, the legs move like an egg-beater – i.e. one leg circles clockwise, while the other moves in an anti-clockwise direction. The lower legs are moved in such a way that the inside of the leg and foot press downwards on the water, thus providing upward thrust. The movement is a continuous one, unlike the form of treading water in which a breast stroke type leg action is used. As it is not an easy skill to master, much practice will be required in order to acquire competency.

Changing from back to front

This is an essential skill, enabling a player to look back down the pool to see what is happening behind his line of vision, before reverting to the front or changing direction completely. Spinning and rotating are also useful skills and **Rotation swimming** (see page 31) is an effective way of practising how to change from swimming on the front to the back, and vice versa.

Fig. 99: Swimming with the ball

Swimming with the ball (see fig. 99)

This requires a modified front crawl stroke, with the head and shoulders raised. The ball is contained between the arms with a high elbow action and is carried on the bow wave in front of the face. Short practices in swimming without the ball may be required first to accustom pupils to this version of front crawl.

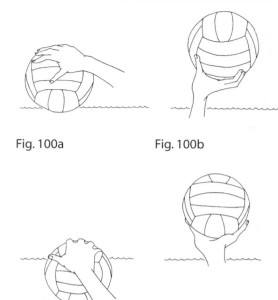

Fig. 100a   Fig. 100b

Fig. 101a   Fig. 101b

Lifting the ball

There are three methods of doing this:
- by placing the open hand under the ball and scooping it up
- by placing the hand with fingers outspread on top of the ball and rolling it until it is comfortably resting in the upturned palm (*see figs 100a and b*)
- by pressing down on the ball so that the upthrust of the water causes it to rise and then to be rotated into the upturned palm of the hand (*see figs 101a and b*).

Pressure on the water with the opposite hand will help to maintain body balance while attempting any of these lifts.

Fig. 102: Throwing the ball

Throwing the ball (see fig. 102)

After lifting or catching the ball, it should be carried backwards in the throwing hand, clear of the water, until it is over the shoulder. It is important to keep the body upright and steady, with the arm almost straight, and to complete the throw with a flick of the wrist. A pass which is caught in the air is called a 'dry' pass. That which is thrown into the water in the pathway of the receiver is called a 'wet' pass and allows the player to continue swimming and to control the ball without having to stop.

Catching the ball

The ball should be thrown so that it reaches the catcher just above head height. It should be received in front of the shoulder and carried backwards to absorb the impact and to prepare for throwing. It is important to watch the ball as it is received.

Shooting

There are three main methods of shooting:

- **power shot** – which should be so forceful that its momentum carries it past the goalkeeper, even though it may be partially blocked
- **bounce shot** – also a powerful shot by which the shooter attempts to bounce the ball off the water, to be deflected into the goal

- **lob shot** – which requires a long, high, arching throw by a player who is relatively unmarked and is a fair distance from the goal. It is used when the goalkeeper is at one side of the goal and when a direct shot might be blocked by opposing players.

PLAY PRACTICES

The water polo skills outlined above can be incorporated in play and small games situations, some of which have been described in earlier chapters.

Individual practices

Spinning top

While treading water, pressure is exerted by each hand in opposite directions and, assisted by an 'egg-beater' kick, the body can be made to rotate.

Rotation swimming

Both front and back crawl are alternated by rotating the body on the recovery of each arm while at the same time maintaining a continuous leg action.

Throw and retrieve

The ball is thrown some distance away, the swimmer goes to retrieve it and turns on to his back to throw again. This sequence may be repeated a number of times.

Lift and shoot

The ball is lifted from the water by various methods already described and a shot is then taken at a target, such as a float or a mark on the poolside.

Partner practices

Throwing and catching
The class is arranged in twos, each couple trying to make as many 'dry' passes as possible in a given time without dropping the ball.

Swim, throw and pass
Whilst maintaining a fair distance apart, partners exchange a series of 'wet' passes, with the receiver moving a few metres away before returning the hall.

Pass and shoot
After exchanging three passes, the one in possession shoots at a target. Alternatively, passing can continue until one partner calls out 'Shoot!' The other partner must then shoot at once.

Group practices

Ball passing
Players are arranged in groups of three or more and are spaced apart at intervals of four or five metres, each treading water. On a signal, a ball is passed from player to player, each group endeavouring to make as many passes as possible in a stated time, without the ball touching the water.

Dribble and pass race
Small teams of players stand in lines, one behind the other and facing across the pool. No. 1 in each team dribbles a ball to the opposite side, turns and throws it back to land in front of no. 2. The same procedure is then followed until the whole team has crossed over.

Wandering ball (2)
The players are arranged in a large circle and two or three go inside. The players on the outside attempt to throw a ball across the circle and the inner players try to intercept. Any successful interceptor changes places with the thrower. The players must tread water and the ball must not be thrown above reachable height.

Two against two
The class is divided into fours. Two of the players with a ball attempt to make as many consecutive passes as possible without the ball being intercepted or touched by the other pair. If this happens, possession is changed. The number of passes is finally compared to see which pair has made the most.

Three passes
This game is exactly like two against two, except that every time a pair make three consecutive passes they call 'Up!' and gain a point. Whenever this happens the game restarts, with possession of the ball going to the other pair. Should the ball be dropped or touched by either of the intercepting pair, possession is changed at once.

Corner spry (3)
In this game the players are arranged in lines, double-arm width apart, facing a thrower some three or four metres away. All tread water. The ball is then passed to each player in turn down the line. When the last in line receives the ball, he dribbles it around the back of the team and becomes the new thrower. The original thrower also swims around the back of the team to become the first in line. The game continues until all the players are back in their original positions.

APPARATUS

Goalposts and nets

Since these are expensive items to buy, goal targets can be improvised by:

- placing skittles or floats on the poolside
- draping towels on the edge of the pool
- standing a hoop upright on the poolside, using hoop stands as supports
- using a bench on the poolside, length-ways on
- having goals painted on the pool wall
- using the full width of the pool and scoring by dribbling the ball to touch the wall.

Water polo caps

Players are usually distinguished by wearing coloured cloth caps. However, two sets of contrasting colours (e.g. blue and white) can easily be made with the co-operation of the school needlework department or of parents.

Water polo balls

A water polo ball weighs approximately 1 pound (0. 45 kg) and has a circumference of between 0.68 and 0.71 metres. Balls are expensive to buy and instead, plastic footballs may be used and will serve the purpose adequately.

Referee's flags

The referee communicates with teams in the water by means of a whistle and coloured flags. The latter can be attached to the ends of a short stick or lengths of round towelling. By rotating the flag the referee can indicate which team should take possession of the ball after a stoppage. (See fig. 107a on page 76.)

Pool markings

The half-way line can be indicated by draping towels or lengths of cloth over the poolside. Alternatively, the centre of the pool could be indicated by placing two or three floats one on top of the other or by putting skittles in position.

8 • Survival Swimming

Once swimmers have reached a certain degree of proficiency, they should be taught a number of survival skills so that they are better prepared should they ever they get into difficulties in water. A good swimmer should not only be able to swim at least a quarter of a mile (400 metres), but also have experienced swimming with some clothing on, be able to demonstrate an understanding of the Water Safety Code and understand the dangers associated with water. However, some of the skills listed below can be taught as soon as children are ready to be introduced to them.

The Amateur Swimming Association has devised a series of Swimming Challenge and Personal Survival Awards which require candidates to demonstrate their ability to perform certain important skills. These include:

- safe entry into water from a height
- treading water
- swimming with light clothing on
- surface diving and underwater swimming
- assuming the HELP position
- participation in the HUDDLE position with at least two other swimmers
- sculling head-first and feet-first
- performing backward and forward somersaults
- climbing out of the pool unaided and without the use of steps or rail.

Since some of these skills, such as treading water and sculling, have already been dealt with elsewhere in this book, this chapter will deal with only those not previously covered.

Safe entry

In an emergency it may be necessary to enter water from a height, so it is important to learn how to do this safely. Wherever possible follow these important guidelines:

- Step off the point of entry. Do not leap or throw yourself.
- Keep the body straight, head up, hands to sides.
- From low heights spread your arms and legs. This will have a braking effect and stop you from going too deep.
- When the water is shallow or of unknown depth, either use a **Tuck jump** (see fig. 86, page 57) or a **Straddle jump** (see fig. 87, page 57).

Swimming with light clothing on

In an emergency, entry into water may have to be made with some clothing on. For the Swimming Challenge Awards the clothing required on top of swimwear is:

- boys – shirt and trousers
- girls – blouse and skirt or trousers.

For the Personal Survival Awards an additional item of clothing, in the form of a long-sleeved jumper, is required. Early practices should preferably be carried out in shallow water, in which pupils are able to stand up. Once confidence has been established, deeper water may be used.

Swimming underwater

The three most common ways of travelling underwater are:

- using the breast stroke action, but with an extended arm pull towards the sides
- using the same breast stroke arm action, but with a front crawl leg action
- extending the arms as in dog paddle and using a crawl-type leg action.

As it is important to see where you are going, the use of goggles is recommended to afford clear vision. Some preliminary breathing practices should precede any underwater swimming practices, to accustom the children to holding their breath without distress. Pushing and gliding to the bottom of the pool and then surfacing is a good way of getting children used to being underwater and holding their breath. Initial practices should be over short distances, carried out in shallow water, and with only one or two children swimming at a time so that they can be kept under close observation.

Fig. 103: HELP position with life jacket

The HELP position

The Heat Escape Lessening Posture (HELP) is designed to conserve heat and also to ensure that no more effort than necessary is expended in order to keep afloat. This is especially important when in open water, where heat loss occurs very quickly.

The position is most easily achieved when a good quality life jacket is being worn (*see fig. 103*) but it can be adapted should some

Fig. 104: Help position with float material

other flotation object (e.g. a large plastic container or ball) be available (*see fig. 104*).

In order to protect those parts of the body which lose heat most easily – e.g. the groin area – the lower limbs should be pressed tightly together, knees bent and upper legs drawn up to cover as much of the abdomen as possible. In this position, the head will be kept clear of the water. Alternatively, the lower legs may be crossed, if this is found to be more comfortable. The upper arms should be then held close to the body so that the forearms are held close alongside the bent legs. The angle of the body in the water will depend largely on the type and positioning of the item being used as a support.

Participation in the HUDDLE position

This is a method of conserving heat when a number of people (three or more) are involved. Again, the effectiveness of the huddle will depend upon the type of material

Fig. 105: HUDDLE position with float material

Fig. 106: HUDDLE position with life jacket

– e.g. lifebelt or floating block of timber – available to the group. When all involved are wearing lifebelts, the best formation is that of a tight circle (*see fig. 105*). It is important that the abdomen and sides of the chest should be protected as much as possible. In this position each member of the huddle can take it in turns to signal for help by waving an arm from side to side above the head (*see fig. 106*).

Climbing out of the water unaided

Mastering this skill in the relative safe conditions of a swimming pool is included in order to provide practice in getting out of the water in an emergency situation, e.g. after falling into a canal or river. Where it is possible to reach the edge it is usually possible to get out of the water by heaving oneself up with the arms, getting a leg over the side and clambering out. Where this is not possible, using a strong breast stroke leg kick whilst treading water will often provide sufficient upward thrust to enable a swimmer to get a grip on the poolside. If the pool is not too deep, submerging and springing off the bottom can also prove an effective way of gaining sufficient height to grasp the poolside.

9 • Presentation

TEACHING A GAME

When first introducing a game or activity, try to avoid lengthy descriptions or time-consuming explanations of the full rules or of the procedure. Instead, as suggested below, provide the detail as the action unfolds:

- announce the activity, using an apt title which need not necessarily be the same as used in this book
- arrange the pupils in their starting positions
- indicate, where necessary, what apparatus the pupils or team leader should collect
- briefly detail the action involved
- give the order to start.

As an example, here is how **One against three** (see page 20) might be introduced.

'This game is called "One against three".

Into groups of four – go!

Now number off from 1 to 4 in each group.

No. 1 drop out and the remainder in each group join hands. No. 1 stands opposite no. 3 and is going to try to touch no. 3 while the others are going to dodge and try to stop him.

Ready – go!'

GAMES LESSONS

There may be occasions when it might be considered appropriate, possibly as a reward for special effort, or as a break from routine, to devote the whole of a lesson to play activity and games. Often referred to as recreational lessons, such occasions provide opportunities for fun and enjoyment, free from the restraints of the more formal lesson situation.

The organisation of this type of lesson depends upon:

- the available space in the pool
- the various depths of water and whether areas can be roped off to separate non-swimmers and swimmers
- the ratio of swimmers to non-swimmers
- the pupil–teacher ratio and the availability of helpers.

Although this applies to all swimming lessons, it is especially important in the recreational lesson because inherently there is more freedom of movement. Obviously, such a lesson requires a great deal of forethought and planning, but based on the previous experience of the pupils and an awareness of their favourite skills, it should not prove difficult to select a wide range of activities and games which all can enjoy, irrespective of ability. While there is no set form to this type of lesson, in order to maintain interest throughout, there should be variety, contrast and maximum involvement. Following a warm-up there should be opportunities for individual, partner and small group activity as well as relays or team games. The three examples given on page 72 are for general guidance only. Teachers and leaders should make their own selections appropriate to their own specific requirements.

(A) Non-swimmers	(B) Swimmers	(C) Mixed ability
Motor boat	Dodge and mark	Here, there, where
Cork collecting	Pushing contest	Jack-in-the-box
See-saw	Swim and dive passing	*Monkey up a stick
Over and under	through hoops	Towing in pairs
Poison	Six ways of crossing	*Towing in pairs
Horses and jockeys	Dribbling relay	Porters' race relay
Push ball	Ten trips	*Waiters' race relay
Corner spry (1)	Target ball	One against three
Scatter dodge ball	Crows and cranes	Newcombe
Crusts and crumbs	Passing in twos	*Team passing

(**A**) Non-swimmers will be in water of standing depth.

(**B**) Swimmers can occupy any area of the pool. However, great care should be taken, particularly in the games situation, that swimmers do not spend too long out of their depth, resulting in over-fatigue. They should be within easy reach of the poolside or near to water where they can stand to rest when required.

(**C**) In the mixed ability group, the non-swimmers and beginners can occupy the shallower water, with swimmers in water approaching the deeper part of the pool. All pupils are performing similar types of activities. Activities marked with an asterisk are the swimmers' equivalent of those immediately preceding.

Activities and games should proceed at a brisk pace and should never be prolonged to the stage of boredom or distraction for some of the group. They should be changed while pupils are still enjoying them, so that they will be keen to return to them at a later date.

SWIMMING GALAS

Swimming galas may be arranged as occasions for providing competition or they may be organised as informal occasions, possibly with guests being invited to observe displays of swimming activity. Some take place annually, while others occur at more frequent intervals.

Swimming galas need not necessarily follow conventional forms based on the four main strokes and catering mainly for those interested in competition. Given a judicious choice of events, a programme can be planned so that as many as possible are able to participate, according to ability and aptitude. Opportunities can be provided for accomplished swimmers to compete with their peers and, at the same time, beginners and those who are more interested in skills of watermanship can also match their prowess with that of others.

On informal occasions several of the activities described in preceding chapters can be included along with orthodox stroke events to allow for wider participation and to add variety to the programme. Also, many of the activities can be used as a basis for a special session, similar in some respects to the 'potted sports' programmes that occasionally take place in the gymnasium, on the playing field or on the athletics track.

For the benefit of those who are unfamiliar with the format of such galas, examples of a mixed programme gala and a novelty programme have been included for clarification. It is not intended, however, that these should be regarded as models to be copied, but rather as suggestions which may be readily modified according to the time available, the pool conditions and, most importantly, the levels of ability of those participating.

NOTES ON ORGANISATION

- When a decision has been taken to hold a gala, those involved should be given the details well in advance and should be asked to indicate on a prepared list the events which they wish to enter.
- As a limit on the number of events in which any one person can take part will be necessary, it is recommended that competitors should be restricted to one stroke event plus one other event.
- A clearly printed list of the events and the names of those who will be competing should then be prepared so that the participants are aware, well in advance, of the order of events and know exactly when they will be required to perform.

Example of a swimming gala programme catering for a class of mixed ability and interest

Event no.	Description of event
1	Beginners' race – one width, any stroke
2	Freestyle race – one length
3	Breast stroke race – one length
4	Plunge competition
5	Back stroke race – one length
6	Sculling race
7	Demonstration of water skills performed by several swimmers simultaneously, e.g.:
	• Submarine
	• Washing tub
	• Porpoise
	• Surface diving
	• Spinning top
	• Canoe
8	Butterfly race – one length
9	Tandem race – one length, in pairs
10	Medley team race – one length per competitor

Note: in the Plunge competition, a time limit of 20–30 seconds should be imposed, at the end of which an appropriately loud signal, e.g. whistle or bell, should be used to indicate that the plunge is over and that it will be measured. A float or skittle on the poolside can easily be moved to show the greatest distance covered.

Example of a gala based on novelty or fun events

Event no.	Description of event
1	Egg and spoon race – one width or one length
2	Balloon race – one length. The balloon must be blown along the surface and should not be touched.
3	Clothes race. Competitors swim halfway wearing pyjamas, undress and carry the pyjamas to the finishing end.
4	Umbrella race. Competitors swim across the pool, collect an umbrella and swim back with it opened up and held above the water.
5	Shunting race (*see page 38*)
6	Lilo or inner tube race. Each swimmer mounts a lilo or large inflated inner tube and covers each lap by paddling with the hands. At each end the next team member takes over.
7	Catching corks competition. A number of corks are thrown into the water. The winner is the first to retrieve four corks, one at a time, and to return them to the starting point.
8	Crocodile race. Four swimmers line up behind a leader, with hands on the hips of the one in front. All use the breast stroke leg action, with the leader using arms also. One member of the team can act as 'cox', calling out the timing, e.g. 'Bend – Kick!'
9	Cup and saucer race. Each swimmer swims across the pool to collect a plastic cup and saucer. This cup is then filled with water and the swimmer returns to the starting point using any method of swimming. The winner is the one who succeeds in doing so without losing any of the water in the cup.
10	Obstacle race. Obstacles, e.g. ropes stretched across the pool, weighted hoops etc., can be used for the swimmers to negotiate while swimming a length of the pool.

- Any apparatus required should be set out in readiness before the start of the gala.
- Whenever possible, arrangements should be made for swimmers to be seated when not participating.
- To ensure that pupils keep warm between events, they should be advised to dry off and to wear tracksuits or other light clothing.
- The emphasis throughout should be on enjoyment, with the efforts of all taking part being given due recognition in the best sporting traditions.
- Time permitting, after the gala proper there might be a brief 'splash session' to allow all participants free time in the water.

10 • Apparatus

Apart from the fact that some non-swimmers and learners may be using such familiar and popular buoyancy aids as arm bands, rubber rings and floatboards, most of the activities and games described require little, if any, equipment. Once pupils have acquired basic water skills, the development of individual play, together with partner and group interaction, can provide a wide variety of interesting and enjoyable challenges. Where apparatus is required, however, it may be quite readily obtainable, as indicated later, or some items may be improvised with a little thought and ingenuity.

SWIMMING AIDS

Inflatable arm bands

It is important that these are snug and well fitting. Double-chamber types are most suitable and those with a flat portion which fit under the arm will allow more freedom of movement than other types currently available.

Inflatable rubber rings

These, also, must be close fitting and there should be no possibility of them slipping down the body. To avoid mishaps, however, a tape can be fitted to opposite sides of the ring and placed over one shoulder as a safety strap. This type of aid allows complete freedom of the arms.

Floatboards

For general purposes a simple rectangular float approximately 76 x 38 cm in size will suffice. The material should be compact, not likely to crumble or absorb water and should be robust. Floatboards can also be used for guided play activity.

Distinguishing markers
- Latex caps, mixed colours
- Fabric sports caps
- Rubber wrist bands, coloured

Games equipment
- Diving bricks, rubber
- Lightweight plastic hoops
- Hoop stands
- Quoits, sorbo rubber
- Floating buoys and quoits
- Slalom games (weighted plastic strips or weighted hoops)
- Weighted hoops
- Playbricks, soft cellular foam
- Floating basketball game
- Mini water polo goals (poolside or floating type) (*see fig. 107c*)
- Mini volleyball game
- Floating rope
- Skittles
- Diving discs
- Weighted toys, e.g. dive frogs
- Water polo balls – Mitre, Mouldmaster
- Table tennis balls
- Referee's flag
- Gamester balls

IMPROVISATION

In the early stages of introducing new games it may be prudent to improvise for a trial period at least, rather than to purchase expensive equipment which may subsequently be seldom used. Those working on tight budgets may find it possible to provide their own items of equipment by using the resources of Handicraft Departments of Schools or Colleges or by seeking the co-operation of parents with DIY skills.

Goals and targets

- Two small piles of floatboards placed on the poolside. Note: in private pools, if the poolside is sufficiently close, water polo goals for practice purposes can be painted on the wall.

- Skittles placed on the poolside. Improvise by using plastic bottles or containers which have been thoroughly cleaned and painted, if required.
- Hoops suspended vertically on two stands (*see fig. 32*). These are purpose-made stands, especially shaped and PVC-coated, obtainable from sports outfitters.
- Hoops tied vertically on DIY stands (*see fig. 107d*).
- Strips of material (e.g. towelling) draped over the poolside.
- Motor tyre inner tubes. These can be inflated and moored at the end of the pool. Note: inflation nozzles must be wrapped and padded to avoid injury through contact.
- Weighted hoops (*see fig. 107e*).

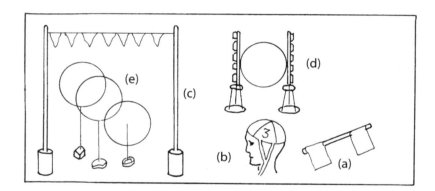

Fig. 107

Appendices

Appendix 1:
Graded Tests for Non-swimmers

The following graded tests may be found helpful to those wishing to assess the progress of non-swimmers. As an incentive to the children being taught, it is recommended that a chart be prepared listing the tests, on which individual successes can then be prominently displayed.

Test • Requirements

1. Place the face in the water and blow bubbles for 5 seconds
2. Place the face in the water and count partner's outspread fingers correctly on two consecutive occasions
3. Walk, holding a float in an extended position, for a distance of 5 metres
4. Hold on to the poolside and perform a recognised leg action (crawl or breast stroke) for 5 seconds
5. Hold on to the poolside, in an extended position, and float face down for 5 seconds
6. Bend down to retrieve a sinking ring or similar object, three times out of any five attempts.
7. From a standing position, push off from the pool floor and glide towards the poolside for 2 metres, holding a flotation aid

Test • Requirements

8. Enter shallow water from a sitting position
9. Push and glide to the poolside, without the use of an aid, for a distance of 3 metres
10. Jump into shallow water from a crouch or standing position without partner support
11. Push off from the poolside on the front, without support, and regain a standing position
12. Holding a float in an extended position, push off on the front and cover a distance of 5 metres, using a recognised leg action (crawl or breast stroke)
13. Push and glide, face downwards, away from the poolside for a distance of 3 metres
14. Push off from the poolside on the back, without support, and regain a standing position
15. Swim a distance of 5 metres using any recognisable stroke, without the use of any aids

Appendix 2:
Kellogg's/ASA Rainbow Awards

The Amateur Swimming Association's Rainbow Award Scheme offers incentives to both beginners and competent swimmers.

CONDITIONS

- These awards are aimed at pupils of 5 years and older and are designed to demonstrate the pupil's ability to swim from A to B without pause and without stress.
- Pupils may touch the side and end of the pool (but not the bottom) in order to turn.

Puffin Award
The ability to travel 5 metres (using any buoyancy aid)

Distance Awards
These awards are designed to test the child's ability to swim the following distances:

Metres	Yards
5	5.47
10	10.94
15	16.40
20	21.87
25	27.34
50	54.68

Metres	Yards
100	109.36
200	218.72
400	437.44
600	656.16
800	874.88
1,000	1,093.80
1,500	1,640.40
1 mile	1,760.00
2,000	2,187.20
3,000	3,280.80
4,000	4,374.80
5,000	5,468.00

More information, as well as details of those eligible to act as examiners, may be obtained from:

ASA Awards Centre
1 Kingfisher Enterprise Park
50 Arthur Street
Redditch
Worcs B98 8LG

Bibliography

SWIMMING

Anyone Can Swim, J. Harrison (Ed.) (Pan Books)
The ASA Guide to Better Swimming, R. Cross (Ed.) (Pan Books)
Swimming, H. H. Smith (Collins)
Know the Game: Swimming (A & C Black)
Swimming – A Handbook for Teachers, H. Elkington (Cambridge University Press)
Swimming – Illustrated Teaching Cards for Schools, Colleges, Swimming Clubs and Parents, G. Austin and J. M. Noble (Primrose Education Resources)
Swimming Teaching and Coaching: Level 1, R. Cross (Ed.) (Swimming Enterprises Ltd.)

DIVING

Better Diving, J. Gray (Kaye and Ward)
Diving Complete, G. Rackham (Faber & Faber)
Diving Instruction (Amateur Swimming Association)

SYNCHRONISED SWIMMING

Synchronised Swimming, H. Elkington and J. Chamberlain (David & Charles)
ASA Handbook of Synchronised Swimming (Amateur Swimming Association)

WATER POLO

How to Play and Teach Water Polo, Charles Hines (Kaye & Ward)
Water Polo Referee's Handbook (Amateur Swimming Association)

Note
All books produced by the Amateur Swimming Association may be obtained from:
ASA Distribution Centre
Unit 2
Kingfisher Enterprise Park
50 Arthur Street
Redditch
Worcs B98 8LG

Index